Miss Manners'
Basic Training™:
Communication

MISS MANNERS'
BASIC TRAINING™

COMMUNICATION

JUDITH MARTIN

CROWN PUBLISHERS, INC.

NEW YORK

Published by Crown Publishers, Inc., 201 East 50th Street, New York, New York
10022. Member of the Crown Publishing Group.
Random House, Inc. New York, Toronto, London, Sydney, Auckland
http://www.randomhouse.com/
CROWN is a trademark of Crown Publishers, Inc.

Printed in the United States of America

Design by Debbie Glasserman

Library of Congress Cataloging-in-Publication Data
Martin, Judith, 1938–
Miss Manners' basic training : communication / Judith Martin.—
1st ed.
Includes index.
1. Etiquette—United States.   2. Communication and technology.
I. Title.
BJ1854.M35   1996
395'.4—dc20   96-24530

ISBN 0-517-70673-3

10 9 8 7 6 5

FOR DAVID HENDIN

The proper way to thank people to whom one is as indebted as Miss Manners is to her family and to Ann Hughey is to write a book so that one may have a fresh page on which to do so.

CONTENTS

Miss Manners' Basic Training™: Communication

CHAPTER 1

BASIC PRINCIPLES

THE PROPER CHOICE OF TECHNOLOGY

When a polite person urgently needs to get the attention of someone who is beyond what we would call shouting distance (if we were not talking about polite people who never shout at one another), what is the instrument of choice?

Voice mail? Pager? Fax machine? E-mail? Overnight express? Footman?

There are not many left in that last category, but Miss Manners remembers vividly when the streets were full of footmen hand-delivering messages. Long after others in the business world wore long trousers or skirts, footmen retained a form of livery; that is to say, they wore short pants as they went whizzing by, with the speedy feet for which their profession was named earnestly applied to the pedals of high-speed bicycles.

Miss Manners leads a quieter life and nothing she has to say, however immortal it may turn out to be, requires others to drop whatever they are doing and heed her words with alacrity at the exact moment she chooses to utter them. Nor does she need to be constantly on call, as are members of the other healing professions. The etiquette business has its emergencies, heaven knows, but it is in the nature of etiquette emergencies that once one realizes what one has done, it is too late. One might as well get a good night's sleep and send flowers with an apology in the morning.

Nevertheless, Miss Manners realizes that other people live

closer to the brink. There are now so many ways of instantly leaving word for someone who is on another line or another system that she had better sort out the proprieties. The issues to be considered before one picks up any of the available instruments of communication are:

How legitimately am I disrupting this person's life? Considering the true urgency of this message—not just the fact that I want to get it out before I forget or go on to something more important—which is the method of sending it that will cause least annoyance?

If the person I need to reach has caught on to the fact that I and others cause disruptions and has taken precautions to thwart my getting right through, need I respect these or may I find clever ways to go around them?

Can I assume that my message will reach only the person for whom it was intended?

The answer to that last question is: Don't be silly. Even aside from the evils of human nature, anything directed at an office may be assumed to be read by others who have the excuse of piously believing that everything arriving at work involves work. At home, it is still a high crime to open letters addressed to others, even others under suspicion of marital treason, but the fancy machines are considered to be family toys open to all.

As for the telephone, it is time to go back to the precautions of party-line days. You may never know if the person to whom you are talking is on a cordless telephone that broadcasts promiscuously, or a speaker telephone, which makes it possible for you inadvertently to amuse whole rooms full of people you didn't know were there.

Screening telephone calls with a receptionist or the humbler answering machine is not a dishonorable thing to do. The warmest people in the world still need uninterrupted time to attend to their lives and should not be outwitted if they have made it obvious that they are not always available upon summons.

E-mail and fax are out for letters of condolence or passion and wedding invitations. Formal communications must not only be written, but written on one's own, not one's employer's, paper.

Casual invitations may be made by telephone, but that so often means leaving a voice message that the advantage of getting an immediate reply is lost and so, probably, are the directions.

It is assumed that others want you to make use of whatever technology they offer—voice mail, for example—but not if it is going to cost them money or tie up their equipment. For that reason, calls to cellular phones should be made and fax messages should be sent only to those who may safely be assumed to be eager, or at least willing, to receive them. Also, the fact that a telephone rings and may disturb someone when a fax is sent should be considered in choosing an appropriate time to send a fax to a private house.

The thought "Does this person really need to hear this?" is a good test before sending any message. Miss Manners is only suggesting adding a second question: "Yes, but right now this very minute?"

AN EXAMPLE

DEAR MISS MANNERS—If the facsimile machine, considered suitable for transmitting legal instruments, is good enough for the courts, is it good enough for Miss Manners?

Specifically, if one pens a note of thanks, in black ink on white writing paper, and sends it in a fax to the home of a gracious host the morning following a hospitable act, is this acceptable? Is this immediate communiqué, made in the afterglow of the event, a fully appropriate alternative to thanks sent by post?

Faster and more advanced yet, what about an appreciation by electronic mail? I have a sense that these modern media ought to be considered informal and/or complementary to posted communication. For example, a friend recently thanked me immediately by E-mail for a wedding gift, then followed up with a conventionally delivered note.

GENTLE READER—You frightened Miss Manners with that opening about what is good enough for the court system. The mere thought that courtroom behavior might provide an etiquette standard for the society scared her half to death.

Once she got a whiff of her smelling salts, she saw that you actually have an excellent feel for the place of fax letters and E-mail in the hierarchy of formality. They fit nicely between written notes and telephone calls, with the faxed letter being slightly more formal than E-mail.

Thus, serious presents, such as wedding presents, and serious hospitality, such as an overnight stay, require serious letters where the seriousness of paper and ink may be experienced firsthand—in other words, by mail, rather than fax. Thanks expressed for trifles can go by fax. E-mail is as informal as a telephone call, but slightly more polite, as it can be taken when the recipient wishes rather than when the sender decides to send it. Thus it is excellent for spontaneous little bursts of gratitude and a supplement to big ones.

It is just as well that we are not in a courtroom. If Miss Manners were to cross-examine you, she would dwell on your point about the advantage of E-mail and faxes as being written in the immediate afterglow. That, of course, is when proper people always write their formal letters of thanks.

ANOTHER EXAMPLE

DEAR MISS MANNERS—Would it be considered rude to send a thank you note by fax to a Human Resource Manager after a job interview?

GENTLE READER—A thank you letter is always nice; the fax is a proper method for delivering business mail to an office; and it's a terrible idea. If you don't want to risk its being seen by someone in the office who had hoped to be promoted into the job you want, put that letter in the mail.

A TERRIBLE EXAMPLE NO MATTER WHAT THE TECHNOLOGY

DEAR MISS MANNERS—From an acquaintance at work, I received a fax headed "A Romantic Valentines Love Story," and reading, in part (spelling corrected):

"Our two Valentines met against near impossible odds and then their love blossomed, despite the 3,000 miles which now separates them both. He had tried unsuccessfully for years to meet a nice woman to date . . . She was at a computer training course and needed a night out to escape the loneliness of her hotel room . . .

"They met accidentally in line at a movie theater, feeling a magnetic pull towards each other when their eyes met . . . In the next three days, they pampered each other with affection. Love letters and faxes kept their romance strong . . . On Valentine's Day, he will fly to her to slip the engagement ring on her finger . . .

"The only sad part of their story is that moving together will be beyond their savings. Our goal is to raise $5,000. If you would like to be part of their love story, they need your help to bring them together . . ."

It is signed by the successful lover himself and I got it from the bride-to-be. The cover sheet notes that I am "free to distribute this true Valentines story to ten of your most romantic friends" and that "no offense is intended in any way by its distribution." What is the proper response?

GENTLE READER—Offense.

Etiquette does not recognize the premature apology. After you have done something ghastly, you may hope to be forgiven by claiming that it was an accident, or you didn't know it was wrong, or you don't know what got into you. But to say "no offense" first only means that you perfectly well realize that you are about to cause offense—and plan to do so anyway.

In this case, there are so many offenses that Miss Manners hardly knows where to begin. Tying up the office fax? Making a charitable solicitation on one's own behalf? Suggesting a chain letter? Intruding one's personal life on others in the hope of personal gain? Buying an engagement ring and then crying that you have no money left?

AN EVEN WORSE EXAMPLE

DEAR MISS MANNERS—Today I received two erroneous faxes at my home fax machine, including extremely private information about the TB and HIV status of individuals who had been tested at one facility and were doing business with another. I often receive faxes of this nature, as the people dialing from different agencies or medlabs transpose numbers, or just have the wrong one.

The fine print on one of today's faxes said that if I wasn't the person for whom the fax was meant, I should phone the lab immediately and mail the fax back. But when I gave the lab the courtesy of a call, a rude and suspicious clerk asked me to fax it back to her. Should I have taken the time just to save her looking it up in her files? I think it should be illegal to fax such sensitive information and would like to encourage workers to take care with privileged information.

GENTLE READER—Miss Manners can hardly wait until the novelty of the fax machine wears off. It is a highly useful gadget in its place, but there are too many people now who can't keep their hands off it.

It's not just wrong numbers, but wasted time. Current standard procedure seems to be to telephone the lucky recipient, either to ask for the fax number or to announce, "I'm going to fax you" and then to get the old machine rattling away on something that could have been said during the call or that doesn't require attention for days or weeks, if ever.

There are other means of communication and it is now necessary to exercise judgment in deciding which is appropriate for which kind of message. Those requiring privacy should not be faxed, even to the right machine. Miss Manners can think of few people who would care to have their medical histories hanging out in plain view of those they know, much less of strangers.

THE PROPER USAGE

Technology likes to play a Catch-Me-If-You-Can game with etiquette. "You don't have any rules for this," it sneers, "because we just invented it." Then it goes tearing off into the future, laughing like crazy, under the cocky assumption that Miss Manners can't catch up.

At the very least, it figures, there has to be a free period in which people can use their new toys to bash one another before ponderous old etiquette comes puffing into sight and, when it can breathe again without wheezing from the exertion, issues directives.

A case in point, just now, is the suddenly popular miniature portable telephone. With the peculiar idea that a mere decrease in size and increase in portability makes the latest telephone appear as something new (and thus bewildering to etiquette), users imagine themselves to be in an etiquette-free zone.

Not so fast, ladies and gentlemen. Do you think Miss Manners has never seen a telephone before? Or that she hadn't heard that some had long since shaken free of their cords (and, in the headiness of freedom, indulged in a lawless tendency to pick up other people's private conversations)? Do you imagine that she is going to spend her life writing new rules for each model that comes along?

It is impossible to invent entirely new human behavior, no matter what the less tasteful movie advertisements seem to promise. Miss Manners hopes she hasn't disappointed anyone by announcing this, but even the most delightfully efficient inventions do not pretend to offer new things to do—only new ways of doing the same things people have always been doing.

Yes, it may be amazing that your mother no longer calls you by sticking her head out back and embarrassing you in front of your playmates—she calls you from her space exploration mission and reaches you sitting in a tree at the neighbors' through the equipment she made you wear on your belt. But it's still your mother calling you. (If you want to talk about human change, forget technology and let's talk about the fact that it might be your father calling you to announce bedtime because your mother's off on that expedition.)

So etiquette really has an easy time of it when asked to make new regulations for new equipment. It need only ask itself what the rules already are for the same behavior.

Interruptions are interruptions, no matter how fancily they are made, and it is normally rude to interrupt people or activities. While it is true that emergencies override this rule, emergencies are, by definition, so rare that they are unexpected.

It is rude to annoy other people with the sounds you make doing business, whether they are fans at a tennis match or people trying to do their own business in the same office.

There has always been a rule against bringing work to social settings. It is, for example, no more acceptable for an executive to use a laptop at a restaurant than it would have been for a secretary to haul a typewriter to the table.

Subtext Alert!

Miss Manners is surely not the only one to have noticed that arguments involving portable telephones soon veer from the actual etiquette question to charges of showing off. Many telephones that are not used to break etiquette rules—such as telephones operated in private cars—are nevertheless attacked by those who may themselves have broken an etiquette rule by looking into other people's cars to see what they are doing. Funny that all these years, Miss Manners never received any complaints about truck drivers using CBs.

This aspect of the situation is irrelevant. Whether or not people are actually doing something important with their telephones or just trying to appear to be doing so is really none of anyone else's business. Besides, Miss Manners has never understood how the telephone came to be associated with importance, or self-importance. Status, it seems to her, is in reaching a station in life where one cannot be easily disturbed.

THE FAX

DEAR MISS MANNERS—I've just got a fax machine and have been sending out lots of letters on it. One of my sisters in England also has fax (much to my amazement) so naturally I sent her one straight away.

I was surprised that she didn't answer by return—hers came the next day. However, she did say that she was in London when mine arrived, hence delay. Which brings me to the point: What is an answer "by return" in the case of fax?

For a letter, it's simple; one should answer if possible by return post. From California, where I live, to England, letters take a minimum of four days, often much longer, so one is fairly safe in allowing a week or so before answering. One has had it dinned into one since childhood that if you get a letter from somebody, you should answer within a week—or max, two weeks. Anything later requires an apology, or rather an excuse even if untrue ("awfully sorry for late answer—I just got back from Alaska/Timbuctoo/etc.") depending on the lateness.

With fax, should one answer within the hour? Or even 15 minutes, given the speediness of transmittal? Perhaps every new technology requires some re-thinking of the correct response. For example, telegrams almost always had bad news; as they were jolly expensive, the answer was simple such as "Desperately sorry. Mitford," only three words. Or if it was just a broken limb, not a death: "Rotten luck. Mitford." Again, only three words; ample, at a shilling a word.

GENTLE READER—As long as ingenious people keep inventing instant ways of attracting other people's attention, humbler ones, such as your own Miss Manners, will have to keep inventing instant ways of holding them off.

Not your sister, of course. And not any of your circle with whom you are on mutually agreeable fax terms. But if you had not understood that the admirable childhood lesson you learned was to be applied selectively, you would now be spending every moment of your life declining with thanks invitations to store sales and expressing written sympathy to fund-raisers for pathetic causes.

Even in social correspondence, Miss Manners dares say you were taught to answer invitations and react to important news with alacrity (not to mention truly impressive thrift), but warned that answering an idly chatty letter by return mail would impose on your correspondent the same courtesy, thus forcing you to exhaust what might otherwise be a lifetime friendship in about two weeks.

The fax note owes less to the letter than to the scribbled note and folded corners or initials on a card when people made morning calls. This, in turn, became the telephone message. Calls of both kinds had to be returned promptly, but not immediately, unless one wished to take the severe measure of ignoring them. The miracle of the telephone answering machine, which the fax machine continues, was to provide a decent way of delaying without prejudice—the polite assumption being that the person wasn't there to receive it, or that the equipment hopelessly mangled the message.

If they ever get these things working perfectly, Miss Manners will have to come up with a better excuse.

THE FAX—PRIVACY

DEAR MISS MANNERS—Exactly how public is a fax message sent to my office and addressed to me? Is it like a postcard (which my mother and the mail carrier brazenly and openly read), or is it like a business letter, which only I or my secretary may open?

A colleague approached me waving my fax—concerning a very sensitive company matter—reading it aloud, unapologetically, and pontificating about what my response ought to be. She has since demanded to know the outcome of this matter, which has no bearing on her job whatsoever.

What to do? Move my desk right beside the fax machine?

GENTLE READER—Postal card rules indeed apply to the fax, but Miss Manners notices that you have the misfortune to be surrounded by people who do not practice postal card etiquette. The rule is that no one must read an open communication, but that no one must assume that everyone else has not read it. Got that?

In other words, no strictly private message should be sent unsealed. And yet it is a transgression of etiquette for anyone to acknowledge having read anyone else's mail, no matter how openly it was sent. So your colleague was polite in delivering the fax, rude in reading it aloud and unspeakable in inquiring about it. Your response should have been, "I believe that was intended for me." As to your letter carrier, Miss Manners cannot imagine why he hasn't died of boredom long ago from reading the inane messages people send from their vacations.

THE BEEPER

DEAR MISS MANNERS—I work as a systems-support programmer for a major computer company. As such, I am often on call, most ostensibly by the carrying of a personal paging device, more affectionately known as a "beeper."

As you are aware, many professionals are likewise blessed in today's time-conscious society. When in possession of said device, I feel awkward both in attending most any gathering (for fear of interrupting the event) and in what is the proper way to excuse myself should I indeed be paged. The beeper has added an element of discomfort and awkwardness to several lives besides my own.

GENTLE READER—Indeed, an increasing number of people seem to be so blessed. Miss Manners is delighted to find one concerned with how not to spread his blessing to friends and bystanders.

The etiquette rule, which is bound to shock modern society, is that business does not, repeat not, take precedence over socializing. If you are being entertained, you may not assume that everyone will understand that you are subject to being called off to save the world. If such is the case, you must plead special indulgence and make arrangements that will not inconvenience others.

First of all, a person on call should not accept invitations to seated dinners, weddings, or other highly structured events in which a premature departure will leave an obvious hole. Miss Manners knows how vital your contribution to society is, but you can still get someone to cover for you during your godchild's christening.

Second, do not carry a noisemaking beeper anyplace where noise is disruptive; silent beepers that vibrate to call attention to themselves are available.

Third, plan ahead so that your exit is unobtrusive. If you are going to the theater, make sure you get an aisle seat; if you are at a large party, slip out with only an apology to the hosts.

Thus we get to the fourth rule: The possibility of an obviously untimely departure from any social event, for no matter how noble a cause, requires an advance warning to the hosts that you might be called away and a profuse apology if you are. Even "I'm terribly sorry—when you work at the White House, your life is just not your own; I hate to leave, but the President insists that I come in this minute for an emergency session" is an offensive statement if the initial apology is omitted.

THE CAR TELEPHONE

DEAR MISS MANNERS—The wealthy have done it again—with today's technology and an embarrassment of riches, they have found a new way to be impolite. These people should be ashamed.

Some people have always treated those of us who serve the public in a most arrogant way, but now, with the popularity of the car telephone, they have found a new means to be discourteous. I, along with uncounted thousands, work at a drive up window and have for years. People have always been impatient while waiting to be served—at times, the line of cars goes nearly around the building—and invariably any delay is blamed on the employees. Many people have not been shy in venting their anger.

I do not wish to be blamed for any delay caused by a customer so engaged in conversation on their carphone that they completely ignore me or hold up their index finger in that universal symbol which means, "I'll be with you in a minute." My time is valuable, too. One customer once told me he was sorry he took so long on his phone, but he makes part of his living that way. What does he think I am doing? Would any customer wish to be ignored while a clerk finished a phone conversation? I think not.

Miss Manners, I believe it is only right that a person show common courtesy and refrain from using a carphone while being helped at a drive-up window. I only ask that you print this letter and perhaps some of these self-centered yuppies will realize just how rude they have been.

GENTLE READER—Miss Manners will do you one better. She will request your employer, and those who manage all drive-in establishments, to formulate a policy to circumvent the rudeness you describe.

The answer to that "I'll be with you in a minute" signal should be the also universally recognized "Pull over there" signal of pointing to a place beyond the service window and a beckoning signal to the car next in line.

In ordinary lines, people who are not prepared to do business when their turn is called are shunted aside so that those who are ready may be served. Surely this would be a sensible system for drive-in facilities. Those who want to use their car telephones without losing their places in line could take the precaution of writing down their orders (or faxing them from their cars to your station) so that they may give them out without interrupting their work.

THE SPEAKERPHONE

DEAR MISS MANNERS—Like many of your readers, I am forced to conduct much of my business through conference calls by speakerphone. Unfortunately, no one seems to know what rules of etiquette might help these calls run more smoothly.

At the beginning of the call, should everyone be notified as to who is on the call? Should parties who get called away on other business notify others when they leave the call and when they return? How does one politely request another party to pick up the receiver to discuss a subject not appropriate for the speakerphone?

GENTLE READER—You have correctly guessed two of the rules and Miss Manners only needs to add that it is proper to say, "We'll discuss this in private" to suggest that it's time to pick up the receiver.

The reason you must warn callers who is present is that it is impolite to listen to someone who does not know you are listening. This is not a new rule. Before the invention of the speakerphone, this rule spent all its time going after eavesdroppers.

THE ANSWERING MACHINE

Can you reach anybody on the telephone? Anybody? Your children? Your dry cleaner? Your lawyer? Your neighborhood movie theater? Your sweetheart? Your government representative?

Apparently not. Miss Manners has heard you snarling away at taped messages, voice mail, beeps, fax signals and other devices that have replaced the human voice at the other end of the telephone. Occasionally, she still hears you trying to argue with the human-voiced but (according to you) heartless receptionist who refuses to connect you with the object of your electronic desires.

Miss Manners has also heard your plea that she sympathize with your frustration and call for a return to the telephone manners of the past that required picking up the telephone when it rang and finding out what the person on the other end of the line wanted. Not a chance.

Miss Manners always hated the custom that granted the telephone perpetual right-of-way. No matter how delighted people may have been at the ability to be in immediate touch with whomever they wanted to call, whenever they found it convenient to call, nobody has ever wanted to live perpetually prey to someone else's notion of a convenient time.

Until recent years only those who could afford to pay people to act as buffers could protect themselves. Now there are so many protective devices available that the power of the telephone—to those who want others to be on call for them, even though they are not willing to be similarly available—has been all but canceled. And until random-dialing telephone solicitation is recognized to be tantamount to housebreaking, there are going to be more and more people who quite sensibly shut themselves off from electronic intrusions.

Fine. Perhaps now that the system doesn't work any more, the shrill demands of the telephone having been thwarted by a series of billable-by-the-month inventions, we can work out a civilized way to get in touch with one another. Miss Manners suggests pausing just a minute before reaching for the telephone, and asking oneself the following questions:

Do I really need an immediate exchange? If I leave a message on the machine, and the person calls back and leaves a message on mine, will we be able to handle the matter just as well as if we had talked? Could we just as well fax each other? Or—for a really radical solution, which is cheaper besides—write letters?

Miss Manners admits that there are times when the conclusion can only be that a true exchange is necessary. In that case, the message system may be used to arrange a mutually agreeable time. She suggests adapting the form that used to be employed for regular, casual socializing in person, when a willing hostess would say, "I'm always home Thursdays," or "We take tea at 4:30, and are always happy to see visitors." The modern equivalent is "The best time to catch me is between 5 and 6," or "Saturday mornings are a good time for me to chat."

It is only fair, then, to use whatever devices are available to keep other callers from bursting in on the line ahead of the one who got there first. The one that Miss Manners uses for that purpose is marvelously simple and all telephone companies offer it—free. It's called the busy signal.

THE CALL-BACK CODE

DEAR MISS MANNERS—A friend of mine has developed the annoying habit of using the telephone code to call the last number that called her phone but did not leave a message.

If she is near her phone but for whatever reason can't answer it, she waits for the person to leave a message. If no one does, she dials the code to find out who called, then informs the person on the other end that they cost her 75 cents because they did not leave a message and she had to use the code service to find out who called.

She has her own business at home, so I can understand her not wanting to miss a call, but her phone message also gives her beeper number. Is it rude not to leave a message? My feeling is that if someone wants to leave a message, they will. What should you tell someone who informs you that you cost them 75 cents because you did not leave a message?

GENTLE READER—Miss Manners is sorry to have to inform you that your friend has gone technology-berserk. There is nothing wrong with using all that equipment, but Miss Manners has noticed with alarm that it seems to exceed some people's emotional capacity.

The sign of having gone bananas is to cease to regard such equipment as a convenience for its users, but to regard people as its servants. This is what this poor soul has done. An answering machine makes it possible for those who wish to do so to leave messages; it does not demand messages. Calling back to retrieve missed calls may be a convenience for the retriever, but her choosing to use it does not entitle her to berate her callers.

Besides, by Miss Manners' calculations, it is your friend who has cost herself all that change, first, by not getting to the telephone on time and, second, by not having the patience to wait for her callers to try again.

THE CORRECT CHOICE

To Miss Manners' mystification, otherwise sensible people are still citing "lack of communication" as the source of all human strife and recommending "more open, honest communication" as the solution to our earthly trials.

As if we hadn't spent the last several decades listening to the entire population freely, honestly, easily, openly and spontaneously communicating its every twinge of ill temper. What do the promoters of ever more communication imagine is being held back?

Is it really something we want to hear?

Miss Manners, in contrast, is alarmed that information technology (for which she is grateful every day of her life) has inadvertently increased the public danger of being hit by barrages of uncharitable frankness. There are too many people with itchy fingers on the Send key. She shall have to put a restriction on the use of E-mail, even though she thinks it the best means of quick communication since the pony express. (Never did much care for the telephone.) New tools require new rules.

E-mail has the great advantage of not having to be fed, although Miss Manners has to give hers a reassuring pat now and then to get it going. But its speed has done away with the old built-in time lags in which to think the communication through, put it in more diplomatic terms, or decide that expressing it will create more trouble than satisfaction.

Here is her ruling:

No heavy emotions may be properly communicated through E-mail or bulletin boards—not to acquaintances and certainly not to strangers. "Flaming," as it is called when vicious messages are unleashed, is the written equivalent of shouting at passersby in the street and should be similarly ignored. E-mail attempts at achieving intimacy are the equivalent of an even worse kind of street remark and should be reported.

Even an E-mailer's intimates, who may be grateful to receive a reaffirmation of previously declared affection, or employees, who may not be grateful to receive measured criticism but at least are not surprised, must be protected from attacks lobbed at them through their own computers. Emotional bombs, including, but not limited to, "Will you marry me?" "I'm leaving," "I'm pregnant" or "You're fired," should not be dropped through the E-mail.

Miss Manners' anxiety arises from her recognition that otherwise polite human beings may occasionally go into a frenzy of anger or of love or a lethal mixture of the two. She is also aware that such passions are inevitably accompanied by the delusion that zinging pithy words will produce remorse, desire, guilt, romantic longing, shame, fear or determination to reform from the object of the message.

This unfortunate idea has been known to attack normally mild people and make them let out streams of sarcasm or unwarranted sentimentality. Neither has a high success rate.

A Sampler of Urgent Communications and the Correct Means by Which to Make Them

. . . showing that not everything should be shouted from the housetops.

"How did you know a yacht was the very thing I wanted most?"

"I can't live without you."

"I send you my deepest sympathy."

"We believe you to be overqualified for the job."

Wedding and graduation invitations and announcements

"We're going to have a baby, darling."

"We have a new baby."

"Congratulations on a great job."

ALL AVAILABLE MEANS

Invitations to dinner parties, receptions, teas, cookouts in the back yard— in descending order of formality

"We had a fabulous time at your party and we hope Brendan is feeling better."

"Megan had to miss school yesterday because of a cold."

"Harriett just won the Nobel Prize!"

ALL AVAILABLE MEANS

"Brendan and I are divorcing by mutual agreement."

 NO OTHER MEANS ACCEPTABLE

"Your AIDS test came back positive."

"The customer hated our presentation this
morning. We have 24 hours to come up
with a new, utterly brilliant idea or we're all
going to be looking for work. Strategy
meeting in Zebulon's office—the whole
A-team—at 2 p.m. sharp."

"Book Group meeting Thursday at 6:30—Read
The Inferno and bring casserole for 12."

KEY

 Handwritten

 Voice Mail

 Engraved

 In Person

 Facsimile

 Greeting Card

 E-mail

 Telephone

Computer

Crayon

Prudent people eventually learn this and, unable to control the outpouring of unattractive threats or pleas for pity, at least force themselves to let rash letters sit overnight to be reconsidered in the morning. The most fortunate are able to consult with trusted friends—who lock them in their rooms until the urge to make fools of themselves subsides.

Even the imprudent and the friendless used to have the advantage of an enforced waiting period. When it was necessary to dip the quill, powder the paper and probably set the letter on fire while sealing it, making it necessary to start all over again; and when there was no use rushing off with the results because there would be a wait before the message would be picked up from postbox or out box anyway, there was a natural cooling-off period.

Not enough of one, of course. A lot of communications still got through that eventually caused regret to their communicators, as well as to those on the receiving end. But now the message is no sooner thought than sent—and often to more people than intended. You can't burn a letter that's already out burning others.

The more emotional the content, the more cumbersome should be the means of conveying it. Highly emotional communications are best made in person, where the effect can be assessed and the message tempered to the reaction.

It is true that they may also be made effectively by letter, if great care is taken over the wording and choosing of paper and ink. Even typing a message in letter form on the computer takes some time to format and print on the right paper. With the unfortunate demise of the typewriter repair shop, Miss Manners can hardly think of putting a stop to that. She can only intone solemnly: Think before you fax.

CHAPTER 2

THE ELECTRONIC WORD

CYBERSPACE ETIQUETTE

The more Miss Manners heard about the excellent concept of "netiquette," the more she kept wondering why it sounded so familiar. The problem that it addresses—how to deal with people who take advantage of unusually open social access to misrepresent who they are, to press unwelcome intimacy, to monopolize others' time, to be nasty without fear of ruining their everyday reputations, to make bores and pests of themselves—seemed like something from long ago.

Miss Manners' memory was oddly mixed with pleasant recollections of sea breezes. Ocean voyages, she realized. Those were the same etiquette concerns as in the days when one was able to cross (as we used to say without anyone's wondering "Cross what?") without fellow passengers' leaning their chairs back onto one's lap. Cyberspace, like the space on the open seas, is free of some constraints that should be observed on land. So in spite of a speed difference, it presents the same difficulties, as well as the same advantages, that come with the freedom of shipboard life.

How can one take advantage of easier social opportunities without risking being subjected to horrid behavior? How can one know whom to trust when isolated from any social apparatus that can supply background information? How can one prevent a few awful people from ruining the ambience for everyone else?

Socializing outside of normal social controls is never as safe as inside them, which is why young ladies used to be warned to beware of those they met on ocean crossings who represented themselves as gentlemen.

Young ladies used to resent the warning. It was just there (as etiquette has ever been taxed with being) to spoil their fun. They could take care of themselves. They didn't need to wait for proper introductions from known people to be able to tell who was respectable and who wasn't. They just knew.

Not always, as some of them—and their modern sisters who brought that attitude to such landlocked institutions as singles bars—unfortunately found out. But the computerized generation (as opposed to Miss Manners' generation, which loves its computers but keeps getting itself into technological difficulties and calling on the young for mercy) has become more sophisticated. It knows that surface clues can be intentionally or unintentionally misleading, that the law cannot monitor all behavior—indeed, that it often should not, even if it could—and that therefore the protection of etiquette is needed. So while in ordinary life, old-fashioned types are still calling for natural, etiquette-free behavior in spite of having lived so long with its consequences, the computer literate are calling for cyberspace etiquette.

Miss Manners is delighted—not only because they are on the right path, but because at last she can offer them assistance. Cyberspace etiquette is, in a way, etiquette in its purest form. No one can guess how old or rich or good-looking or stylish anyone is; people can be judged only by the way they represent themselves. But because everyone is, or can be, anonymous, the punishment of community disapproval or banishment is handicapped. A wrongdoer can merely disappear and return under a different identity.

So the only reason to be polite is that cyberspace social life, like all forms of community life, doesn't work as it is supposed to unless participants voluntarily restrain themselves from spoiling it. The vocabulary may be different—flaming for insulting, writing in capital letters for shouting, spamming for buttonholing huge numbers of people—but the rules should be familiar to anyone who engages in ordinary social life:

Newcomers should introduce themselves and then study the interests and habits of any group they wish to join. Some chat groups, like some individuals conducting E-mail correspondence, are highly focused on a particular topic and impatient with irrelevancies and repetitions; others are intended for companionship and less particular about the content.

The tone also varies from rough to refined. Just as speech and behavior are supposed to be different in locker rooms than in drawing rooms—although you'd never know it from some of today's drawing room conversations—cyberspace has areas in which salaciousness or flaming are permitted and ones in which they are offensive.

Whatever the setting, it has always been rude to bore people, to hog the floor, to conduct a private conversation in front of others and to push commercial wares in social settings. It always will be, no matter how new the conditions. Miss Manners accepts no pleas of ignorance about such matters. Nor should those who are the victims of rudeness. Cyberspace society may not be able to identify its miscreants, but it can trace their origins and warn the innocent to stay away from their advances. Toss them overboard, she would advise if she weren't too polite.

OFFICE E—MAIL

DEAR MISS MANNERS—Since the company I work for installed a network linking all the PCs, some intracompany communication that used to occur over the telephone or in memorandums now takes place in the form of electronic mail. E-mail seems to be less formal than a memorandum, more concise than a telephone call and delivered faster than sending a handwritten note through the intracompany mail.

What is appropriate for the tone, style and level of formality in business electronic mail? Some people have personalized their e-mail by making the background and text different colors (blue type on a bright red background). Other people use emoticons such as this: :-)

GENTLE READER—If Miss Manners tentatively approves of emoticons (she confesses that she rather likes the word), will you promise not to take advantage of her innocence and lead her to repeat one that might be naughty?

Not being naughty is, in fact, the chief rule about office E-mail. Office informality is not like social informality, because you are supposed to have a pretty good idea of how much naughtiness your friends find nice. In the office, naughtiness comprises not only what anyone who sees it might find offensive—which covers a lot of territory, since you never know who might see it and who might find what offensive—but overfamiliarity. You are not supposed to get too personal or too cute.

You would not be wrong if you pointed out that this eliminates *any* informality—if you understand informality to mean the relaxing of standards. Relaxing standards of professional behavior in one's place of employment is a truly disastrous idea. (When Miss Manners speaks of varying degrees of formality, she means the different forms that go with different degrees of solemnity. Thus, the message that the company has doubled its profits, or is dissolving, should not suddenly appear on everyone's E-mail. And "Nice job!" from the boss carries less weight—and less chance of a salary raise—when it appears on E-mail instead of a letter.)

On the other hand, cheerfulness is especially prized in the office, where it tends to be rare. In E-mail, which you aptly characterize as the least formal way of writing an interoffice note, a certain amount of breeziness could be charming. Miss Manners has no objection to using color or other resources of the computer for this purpose, provided basic professionalism is preserved. This includes dropping icons that are beginning to get on people's nerves, which is why Miss Manners dearly hopes that the smiley face is headed for well-deserved retirement.

A PROPER REPLY

DEAR MISS MANNERS—When I was promoted to being a vice president, I received congratulatory notes and E-mail from my colleagues at the bank where I work, along with congratulatory phone calls.

Unless I specifically had to contact one of these colleagues for business-related reasons, I did not call back to acknowledge receipt of the notes or E-mail. Should I have somehow replied to each communication, although I would probably not have to deal with these colleagues any time soon?

GENTLE READER—Please tell Miss Manners that you are not suggesting that it is unnecessary to thank people for their kindness when you do not need to draw on their goodwill. Please! Please tell her that you are only wondering whether congratulations need to be acknowledged (yes) and how (the same way they were sent—mail or E-mail).

COMPUTER BULLETIN BOARDS (PART ONE)

DEAR MISS MANNERS—I subscribe to several computer bulletin boards, one professional, one political, two religious and others related to hobbies. I probably spend no more than two hours a week on them, reading what others might say, sometimes posting a comment or question, but often saying nothing.

The discussions are not personal, although sometimes something personal comes out. I like the bulletin boards because I can exchange ideas, information, comments, questions and answers with other people whom I would not otherwise have a chance to speak to on subjects of mutual interest and with whom I might have nothing in common except one area. I have no other responsibility for personal or social interaction with these people, nor they with me. I think most users like it this way.

But some people play by different rules. I have received messages from women who want to meet me. One was visiting from out of town and wanted to have dinner. Another has discovered that we live in the same town and is working up to arranging a meeting of some kind. These women do not have enough personal information about me at this point to know my marital status, my age, or whether I am a drug addict or an ax murderer.

It happens that I am gay and I don't have any interest in spending an evening with a strange woman. I don't use the computer to meet men, either. I told one woman I preferred not to meet people on the bulletin board and she did not pursue it. I don't know if that was rude or not.

GENTLE READER—Miss Manners would not go so far as to say that a computer bulletin board exchange constitutes a proper introduction, but she will say that she has heard of worse ones. Notwithstanding, it does not confer any social obligation.

You need only politely decline whatever invitations are offered. No explanation is necessary, but if you feel it would be more gracious, you could say, "I feel that anonymity is the charm of chatting this way."

COMPUTER BULLETIN BOARDS (PART TWO)

DEAR MISS MANNERS—On an electronic bulletin board, it's considered bad form to stray too far from a conference topic.

In the "Word Processing" conference, you don't want to wade through messages about graphics programs, printer doors, or the President's Middle East policy.

Most of us accept this rule and realize that our message about graphics, printers, etc., will find a more willing audience in conferences under those titles. There's even a "Miscellaneous" conference, where anything is welcome. When we can't resist the urge to stray or to reply on a personal note, we usually make the message "Private," allowing only the sender and the receiver to read it. Others would only know that this private dialogue is going on if they go to a list of all messages and see some marked "Private." These people might feel that they are being snubbed.

Which is more socially incorrect? To violate the sanctity of the conference topic by posting non-germane responses? Or to carry on a private dialogue that excludes others? Both? Neither?

GENTLE READER—Miss Manners has a hard time picturing the disconsolate people who are feeling personally snubbed by not being allowed to read absolutely everything electronically available. On the other hand, she has no trouble at all picturing people who are annoyed at wading through irrelevant material to get to what they had a right to expect. Miss Manners, like you, would prefer people to observe the rules. But she votes for sparing others, rather than intruding on their time.

USENET

DEAR MISS MANNERS—I am investigating setting up a local film usenet on a new computer network as an extension of my classic/foreign film discussion group that meets once a month at the local art and culture center. The club president and discussion leader encourage politeness and respect for the opinions of others while welcoming thoughtful points of view after a showing of the film-of-the-month.

A usenet, short for users' network, is like a computer discussion group or forum where people can read messages, post messages and reply to the messages posted by others. Unlike electronic mail, where the message can only be read by the person to whom it is directed, messages can be posted or read by anyone accessing the forum. How can I foster the characteristics of politeness and respect?

GENTLE READER—What you are proposing is a club—an assembly of people who agree to certain rules of behavior in order to foster the activities and atmosphere upon which they have agreed.

Even Miss Manners notices that this is not as easily organized as a golf or sewing club. You do not need to worry about finding a meeting place or time and nobody is likely to get sick on the rug, but it's harder to interview prospects, bar admission or throw people out.

Hard, but not impossible. Nobody has to belong to a club, but those who do must agree to obey its rules. So the first thing you must do is to post the rules. Welcome to the etiquette business. Typically, usenet rules include bans against remarks that are repetitive, commercial, vulgar, irrelevant, verbose and personally derogatory, but the beauty of a club is that you can set whatever standards you want. Flaming may be ruled out entirely or it may be kept within specified limits or encouraged as good sport.

Some usenet groups ask for facts without opinions; yours, Miss Manners gathers, solicits opinions. The danger is that people will give their opinions of other opinion givers, rather than only of the films. For this reason, Miss Manners particularly recommends a directive that the polite way to say, "How can you be so stupid?" is "I'm afraid I must disagree with you."

Prospects should be asked to review the rules and agree to the conditions. The sensitive among them will not offer contributions until they have read enough to understand the tone that is expected. Those who flout the rules must be asked to leave—or even barred from entering. That, at least, is more easily accomplished by an electronic refusal to accept messages from the exile than if that person is literally banging on the club door.

THE COMPUTERIZED ADDRESS

DEAR MISS MANNERS—Responding to a lovely birthday present I received through the mail from my brother and sister-in-law, I pulled up my brother's existing address from my computer and laser-printed it directly on the envelope. Unfortunately, the address contained my brother's ex-girlfriend's name, instead of that of his wife.

This has been a sensitive issue in the past, both because (thankfully) his wife is very different from his ex-girlfriend and because the error apparently happened frequently when they were first dating, due to similarities in the two women's names.

The gift was especially appreciated because we normally exchange only simple notes and telephone calls. I am quite certain that my brother's wife was responsible for choosing and sending it. My error occurred in my rush to address and mail them an elegant card and personal message of appreciation. Normally I address all correspondence to them by hand, so I hadn't updated the computer information for several years—since before his marriage.

I should mention that my sister-in-law has been a wonderful addition to the family. She is warm and loving and has done her best to instill culture and refinement in my brother who was perhaps (until now!) the least decorous among us five siblings.

I have since received an angry note from my brother, written on my envelope, reminding me of his wife's name. I have learned my lesson about the improper use of my computer for personal correspondence, but what shall I do to correct my error?

GENTLE READER—Grovel.

Grovel, grovel, grovel.

It is one of the oddities of etiquette that a transgression so easy to make and so devoid of ill intent is so grievous. People are forever getting names wrong, for a lot less technologically advanced reasons than you supplied, but even the most forgetful will be furious at anyone's getting that person's own name wrong.

In this case, Miss Manners knows groveling will work, because it has already worked on her. Your letter to Miss Manners has amply documented your eagerness to please, your remorse over your mistake, your admiration and fondness for your sister-in-law and your gratitude that it was she, and not her predecessor, who married your brother. Thus, however you send your communications, content can still triumph over technology.

THE COMPUTERIZED LOVE LETTER

DEAR MISS MANNERS—Is it proper to use a computer for very personal letters? They will be readable and legible, but I shudder to think that one day an ex-lover, when asked if he had any old love letters, will pull out my printouts and disappoint his audience.

Then again, love letters aren't meant to be framed and put on display for beauty, but to be read. I have very poor handwriting—a learning disability I have always had but have found ways around. I use a portable laptop for taking notes in class and for personal correspondence.

GENTLE READER—Really good love letters are meant to be pressed to the heart and kissed, after which they become illegible anyway. Miss Manners isn't sure that they are not better off being indecipherable during and after the romance. But surely you are in a better position than she to know whether this gentleman's heart would become more inflamed by exposure to your clarity or to his imagination.

THE COMPUTER SNOOP

DEAR MISS MANNERS—Oh, Sapient One, but how then with those so indelicate as to behold over one's shoulder upon a computer screen what surely they would never transgress, were it already printed out.

The modernity of the problem has left me, and perhaps others, in need of a modern solution. I tire of extinguishing the screen, though this reaches my ends, and communicates my intent, however itself indelicate.

GENTLE READER—Miss Manners first considered your form of address. Let us say she has decided not to disavow it.

Now to the problem: How fortunate it is that modern problems arrive complete with modern solutions. While it is indeed rude to read another's computer screen, Miss Manners assures you that it is not at all rude to make this impossible by turning off the monitor. The polite excuse, if you feel obliged to give one, is that leaving work unattended while you pause to see what your visitor wants of you burns the screen. For just this reason, we have the screen saver. Then the only problem is to recall your hypnotized visitor back to life rather than letting him follow the patterns about until queasiness sets in.

FORM LETTERS

When Miss Manners hears the word "personalize," as in "We want to personalize our announcements," or "Surely you want to have that personalized," she gives off an involuntary, barely perceptible shudder. Something mildly vulgar is about to happen.

Now why should she feel a Bad Taste Alert over such a sympathetic concept? she asks herself. (People who happen to spot her alone on her porch swing, sternly interrogating herself in this fashion, begin to have questions of their own.) Miss Manners is certainly not on the side of the impersonal. She would not want important occasions and treasured possessions to be bereft of touches associated with the actual people involved.

But "personalizing" is so—impersonal. The term is most often used when the intent is:

To fake individual attention on something which has been mass-produced;

To make a mess of a tradition that is perfectly coherent the way it is; or

To aggrandize the individuality of the sender by sacrificing individual attention due the recipients.

Faked individuality is epitomized by the computer letter which cleverly inserts a name into the middle of the text, so that the person addressed thinks, "Gee, they could have put my name at the top of a form letter, but if they put it in the middle, this must really mean that they wrote the whole letter just for me."

The trouble is that there is no one left who thinks that. Miss Manners must have greater faith in the intelligence—and suspiciousness—of the public than those who send such letters. She figures that it took the first recipient about six seconds to figure out that it was a form letter, three seconds to admire the technique and perhaps a few minutes to find out, from the nearest child who had taken computer programming, how it was done. The ploy fools no one.

If commercial enterprises nevertheless want to go on believing in the effectiveness of such personalization, Miss Manners does not want to disillusion them. She does want to disillusion anyone who thinks that the technique can be used to fool friends into believing that they are being treated—as friends, which is to say really individually.

Miss Manners does understand that there are grand occasions when one must address one's friends all at once. There are legitimate social forms for mass mailings, such as wedding and graduation invitations and announcements. The very standardization of these conveys the dignity and formality of the occasion.

The personal part is supposed to be the names, which tell you which individuals are participating in the tradition and even the dates on which they are doing so. Messing with the traditional forms by adding cute touches only undercuts the formality of the occasion, suggesting that one is not really taking it seriously. It also incidentally demonstrates how standardized and limited are the ways in which people reach for originality.

What discourages Miss Manners most, and what is responsible for that delicate shudder, is the spirit in which they do so. Any personalized mass mailing must, by necessity, skip being tailored for the person who receives it. The prime example is the mass Christmas letter, which states everything personal about the writer without regard to how much the recipient already knows or might find of interest.

Adjusting the standard form or even writing one's own form for mass mailing does not achieve a personal touch. When formal announcements are not warm enough for intimates, they should be supplemented with notes or telephone calls saying, "Guess what?" or "You've got to be there." Or the formal can be skipped altogether in favor of the personal announcement, personally written, in the writer's personal handwriting—"We have a new daughter," "I'm finally graduating," "I want you to be the first to know."

Miss Manners is puzzled about why it seems so hard to realize that the way to personalize things is to do them personally.

CUSTOMIZING

Dear Miss Manners—Due to new employment plus more social life, my daughter has less spare time. So now she sends the same computer print-out type letter to all her relatives and friends. She and I had mail corresponded for about 25 years. Our one-on-one question and answer letters are history and so is our feeling of closeness.

Frankly, those form type letters are a turn off for me. I couldn't care less about people's social or material status. Only about feelings, health, relationships, etc., one on one. How do you rate the new future wave corresponding, etiquette-wise?

Gentle Reader—Surprisingly highly. But if you ask Miss Manners how she rates daughters who, busy or not, downgrade their relationships with their mothers, the rating is not so high.

The computer offers a marvelous way of mass-mailing bits of news, jokes and other such delights to several people at once. But to keep the thing polite, Miss Manners requires one of the first two following procedures, plus the third:

1. Write individual letters, in which the paragraphs that would interest more than one recipient are embedded in letters that are, or at least appear to be, custom-tailored to them. This takes a bit more effort than keying in "Dear" at the top with a space for a name. The test is whether the person who gets it can detect that it is a mass mailing.

2. Frankly label the contribution as a widely distributed note, presumably of interest to a number of people. At best, such a communication can only be considered a supplement to whatever correspondence is appropriate.

3. Refrain from using it in place of required correspondence, such as personal letters to your mother.

POOR FORM

DEAR MISS MANNERS—I'm a great fan of computers (I'm using one right now) but I don't think they should be used to write thank you notes. Do you think I'm too old-fashioned when I'm offended by the one I received from a recent graduate? It was obvious that the writer merely changed the name of the gift in each copy and signed his name. The address on the envelope was also typed. Surely, even in our computerized world, this is going too far.

GENTLE READER—Thank-you letters should be written by hand. Miss Manners, who does not consider acts of kindness subject to fashion, grants exemptions only to people with specific physical disabilities that prevent them from writing. Those who claim illegible handwriting should be home practicing their penmanship instead of bragging about it.

Even if the beneficiary of your generosity had one of those exemptions, that letter would have fallen seriously short of being polite. When one cannot handwrite such a formal letter as an expression of thanks, one must supply an apology.

Also, the fact that it was a form letter should have been disguised. One reason Miss Manners is also a fan, as you call it, of computers, is that they make it so easy to customize a basic letter. That graduate should have learned to insert into the letter a description of the specific present you gave and a kind word or two that would apply specifically to you.

CHRISTMAS LETTERS

DEAR MISS MANNERS—Should computer print-out letters that are sent in Christmas cards be to casual acquaintances or close family and friends?

A family member who said she was too busy to answer my letters—at one time, I considered our relationship close—sends me a print-out of all the events of the past 12 months. If they are that important, why not write about them during the year? We all live in a busy world and really cherish our spare time, but are these copied "letters" the way to keep a friendship alive?

Gentle Reader—Miss Manners thought she had dealt with this problem back in the days when Christmas newsletters, being mimeographed in smudgy purple letters, were unreadable anyway. Thus, the recipients were mercifully spared being subjected to information that was immodest, embarrassing, ridiculous or a special holiday concoction of the three.

However, the advent of the computer letter alters the situation somewhat. Somewhat. The basic rule still stands: Mass mailings are suitable neither for those who ought to be kept informed of family events when they happen, nor for those who are not kept so informed because it can easily be guessed that they couldn't care less.

One's entire circle should be informed of births, marriages and deaths as they happen; close friends and relatives may be told of vacations, promotions, the triumphs of children, health problems and philosophical insights. But they should not be mixed. As one Gentle Reader put it, "I feel violated and stunned that someone would have the insensitivity to send us a Christmas letter in which her mother's death is mentioned right before the family trip to Disneyland, and the visit of some children is noted with 'their mom, our friend, is ill—cancerous.' Treating her mother's death so flippantly sickens me, and it is absolutely none of her business to tell everyone her friend is fighting cancer."

It may also safely be assumed that nobody who would be puzzled, if not annoyed, to receive a call that you bought a new car or have expensive dental problems wants to hear about these by mail. With the computer, even the only mildly dexterous among us can manage to pick up only selected paragraphs, add personal inquiries and so on. Had your relative mastered this, she would have been able to send you a letter filling you in on the family details and gracefully interspersed with references to your own family, without having to admit that she was cutting corners.

CHAIN LETTERS

DEAR MISS MANNERS—For the past year, I have been battling cancer and unpleasant side effects from the treatment. During that time, I would estimate that I have received ten chain letters. I'm sure that the people who sent letters promising good fortune to those who copied them and mailed them on to other unfortunates had only my best interests at heart. But frankly, even if I had had the energy and ability to run around xeroxing and mailing out the required number of copies, I would never put such a burden on an unsuspecting friend.

I believe that it is rude and inconsiderate to put one's friends in such a position. Perhaps the people sending them aren't terribly fond of me. Clearly, they are not proud of their participation, or they would include their return address or a friendly note. I would love to know your opinion of chain letters and how you believe they should be handled.

GENTLE READER—Chain letters should be handled as little as possible. A quick gesture, made as soon as one recognizes the nature of the communication, is all that is required to convey them from desk to wastebasket. But Miss Manners is grateful for your reminder that these letters can be hurtful as well as silly.

CHAPTER 3

THE SPOKEN WORD

GENERAL TELEPHONE THEORY

By the sound of the beep, Miss Manners expects you to have mastered the manners to go with all that telephone equipment you are so proud of owning.

If you hate telephones, that's all right, too. There is nothing rude about not taking calls or leaving messages and there are some wonderful alternatives. Miss Manners employs both quill pens and fax machines with about equal dexterity and is looking into the pigeon situation. But unless you resolve never to deal with the system at all, you must learn how to use it to make yourself clear without annoying others. Apparently even the goal of clarity cannot be taken for granted.

"It is almost impossible to hear my parents on their cordless phone," writes a Gentle Reader, "due to a constant buzzing sound in the background so discernible that when I pick up the phone and hear it, I say 'Hi, Mom.' I cannot manage a civil conversation, but they won't replace it or try relocating the base. My feeling is that the buzzing phone is a smack in the face of anyone who wants to speak with them, and I'm within my bounds to tell them I can't talk to them on that phone."

Yes, provided you shout, "Can't hear you! Can't hear you!" before disconnecting. And you would do Miss Manners a favor by writing your parents an occasional love note, just to show them it isn't they but the telephone.

When you are recording a statement for your telephone, it is no longer necessary (Miss Manners has decreed) to give elaborate instructions and it was never necessary to provide entertainment. The machine serves the purpose of a private butler or a professional receptionist and it should answer accordingly, with restrained dignity.

Socially, a somewhat stilted form is permitted for such third parties, in contrast to a person who picks up the telephone and just says, "Hello." The butler-answering machine version is "Mrs. Merriweather's residence," thrilling because it contains the only nonpretentious use of the word "residence." (Speaking of pretentious, Miss Manners knows the whole family lives there, and you may drop the "Mrs.," but by tradition the lady of the house is its spokesperson, so to speak.)

Those who are wary of giving their names to chance callers may merely restate the number. Business messages should state the name of the company. The rest of the message is just "Please leave a message," with no explanation of how devastated you are to miss the call, or misleading promises about when you will call back.

Above all, Miss Manners suggests that anyone who makes telephone calls these days must memorize his or her own full name (you are not the only Sean or Philomela they know), any additional identification and telephone number, so as not to be overtaken by stage fright.

Here is a message reported by a Gentle Reader who decided not to return "a long distance call from a stranger who, for all I know, could be a crank caller or someone trying to sell me swamp land: 'I, I'm not sure if I reached, um, um, the right— is it Lila? Leela? But anyway, uh, my name is ———— and, um, you can, uh, I can be reached, uh, um, through Information, I guess, um, in, um, you can get me through Information in Kansas City, Missouri.' "

To which Miss Manners can only reply: "Beep!"

THE LONG–DISTANCE CALL

DEAR MISS MANNERS—I go to church for some peace of mind. I don't understand why people bring their beeper/phones to this sacred place. These go off in the middle of the prayers, and one loses concentration. I have approached the minister, but with no success. Am I being unreasonable? One lady even accused me of being hostile towards her husband because he carries a beeper.

GENTLE READER—Miss Manners has heard many a claim of why it is more important to talk to one person over another, but this is the first time she heard what God's place is in that hierarchy.

God is apparently the one to be put on hold while one takes a more important call. It seems odd to Miss Manners that a minister of God would acquiesce in this. She suggests that you pursue this matter, perhaps in an open discussion with the congregation, so that a policy may be made in which prayer is respected.

Members of the congregation who may be, in a rare emergency, summoned during prayer to do God's work (not, as is more likely, their own) should have a church office number to give out. The person stationed at that telephone could then enter the sanctuary quietly and tap the needed person on the shoulder without bothering other worshipers. Perhaps there should be a special section at the back for people who plan to combine work and worship.

THE INTERNATIONAL CALL

DEAR MISS MANNERS—As my date arrived at my pied-à-terre for a dinner party in honor of two of our dearest friends who have just announced a blessed event, her cellular phone rang.

For more than a quarter of an hour, she proceeded to conduct business with a colleague calling from Hong Kong.

While I understand that international business pays no attention to clocks, it was a strain for me to toss the salad and speak to my other guests in whispered tones as she carried on with matters of the day. What should one do about cellular calls received after business hours have closed in the recipient's time zone?

GENTLE READER—The simple rule that one should not go out partying until one is off work for the day seems to outrage a great many important people. Miss Manners knows just how important they are, because they tell her. "If I went by *that*," they say, in righteously indignant reaction to her little rule, "I'd never get to relax!" With people who are all that important—even though this category now includes practically everybody—the whole world has a stake in their being able to relax. If they were not in the best of health and moods, they would not be able to make those essential round-the-clock contributions to humanity.

Miss Manners will therefore relax the rule. But not much.

Although people who have basic work to do during the evening should not accept social engagements, everyone is allowed a very occasional exception, provided the agreement of his or her hosts is obtained beforehand. Thus your friend could have replied to your invitation by saying, "I'd love to be there, but I'm expecting a call then that I'll have to take, for about fifteen minutes."

This would give you the choice of saying that you were sorry to miss her but would invite her again when she was less busy, or of saying, "Come anyway. You can just slip in the bedroom with the call when it comes and we'll go ahead with dinner."

If you choose to do the latter, both your date and you should make the interruption as inconspicuous as possible. She should briefly excuse herself and then as briefly apologize upon her return to the party. Only the cynical would imagine that thus removing the showiness from doing important business in front of people who have nothing more compelling to do than to be sociable might cut down on the amount of business being done at parties.

THE CELLULAR TELEPHONE

Miss Manners understands that for the owners of portable telephones the number-one etiquette hazard is embarrassment. There is hardly any more public wallflower than the person who is obviously lugging around telephone equipment that never seems to ring. No one should have to be stuck with having to talk to the person he or she is actually with.

It is, of course, Miss Manners' duty to sympathize with all etiquette problems. But she allows herself some discretion about which ones to suffer over first. In the matter of peripatetic telephones, she worries first about the nonusers present who are being annoyed.

Etiquette favors people who are actually there in the flesh over disembodied voices—a principle that most telephone devotees have failed to master. Not even greed seems to be strong enough to allow businesspeople to ignore the unknown and tentative propositions represented by a ringing telephone in order to accept real money from actual customers on the scene.

In protecting the rights of those who are either disturbed or ignored by wandering telephoners, Miss Manners does not intend to validate the complaints of people who are offended merely by the existence of the equipment, whether or not its use affects them. Anyone who wants to work in an airplane, a hairdressing establishment or while standing in line at the bank has Miss Manners' blessing. The offense is not talking on the telephone, much less in owning the equipment with which to do so. It consists of intruding on others, or neglecting others, in order to do so.

You wouldn't think that Miss Manners would have to tell people not to bring telephones to concerts and parties. But that's only because you have not received the reports she has and still have faith in the ability of your fellow citizens to exhibit a modicum of taste.

It is not only the noise, as in the case of a concert, that violates propriety. Many gatherings, including all social events, are spoiled by being turned into obvious places of business. Unobvious business isn't supposed to be conducted there either, but one would have to commit the error of eavesdropping to make sure conversations were not taking a commercial tone. Any equipment—not only fancy stuff, but papers as well—is out of place.

A person dining in a restaurant alone would technically be allowed polite usage of the telephone, which would be a grave offense if there were another person at the table. But then, it might be considered rude of such a person to take up a table at all while others want to dine—because that pesky old rule about not talking with one's mouth full still applies.

CALL WAITING

DEAR MISS MANNERS—What is more rude, Call Waiting or a busy signal?

I canceled my Call Waiting because I felt that it was a rude interruption during my telephone conversations. Then my mother-in-law got upset because it took her "over 15 minutes" to get through to me. I apologized and my husband flipped. He says it's our phone. We pay the bill, and we can talk as long as we want. Where do you stand? Is there a time limit I should put on my phone calls?

GENTLE READER—Call Waiting is ruder than the busy signal, but Caller Impatient, to which you have been subjected, is even ruder than that.

Call Waiting is rude because it wastes the time of someone who had already been engaged in conversation. However nicer it may appear to deliver a busy signal personally than mechanically, it sets up another rude situation: The person called is expected by both parties to choose which of the two calls is more important, both parties are put off at least temporarily, and whoever loses is miffed.

Caller Impatient only confirms this outrageous expectation by chastising people who do not always hold themselves available to talk the moment they are called. Your mother-in-law is far from the only person to say, "I've been trying to reach you" in injured or accusatory tones.

As your husband says, it is your telephone. Certainly, you can talk on it as long as you want. You may not want to keep apologizing, but neither do you want to take the next step, to what your husband is doing—flipping. A cheerful "Oh, yes, I was having an interesting conversation with a friend" is all you need to reply before beginning normal conversation with the second caller.

CALL FORWARDING

DEAR MISS MANNERS—I gave a party at which four guests put their home or office telephone systems on the Call Forwarding mode to my telephone, only one of them having asked my permission. Throughout the evening, I spent too much time answering my telephone on behalf of my guests, since I do not have paid help for my at home entertaining. I seriously doubt that any of the calls were urgent. Short of taking my phone off the hook, which would really not be wise, I am unable to come up with a non-alienating solution, but I must cease to be an answering service when I entertain.

GENTLE READER—As it is rude to give the telephone precedence over live human beings actually present, the gracious solution would be to say, "Oh, let's just let it ring—I don't want to interrupt our wonderful conversation." If this doesn't discourage guests from forwarding their nonessential calls, it will at least force those who do feel their calls are urgent to do the answering.

*69

DEAR MISS MANNERS—With the advent of Caller ID and Star 69, I receive callbacks from people for whom I have not left messages. They don't know whom they are calling and, suspecting the worst, don't follow the normal courtesy of identifying themselves.

I can understand why they don't, as the people who pay the outrageous price for these services tend to be experiencing harassing calls. Nevertheless this leads to uncomfortable exchanges that poison the calls and relationships, aside from being plain embarrassing. What is the polite way to begin such conversations, both for those with this service and their unfortunate friends who receive their calls?

GENTLE READER—Miss Manners was just about to join you in expressing indignation against people who do not apologize for their dialing mistakes when she noticed a small flaw in your story. You might be one of them.

Presuming those services are working, how did these people get your number? You called them.

So either you want to reach them, in which case they have saved you the trouble of calling back (as well as of leaving a message), or you realized you had misdialed. In the latter case, it would be you we were talking about who rudely failed to apologize when it became apparent that you had troubled a stranger.

This does not excuse callers-back from opening with anything other than the polite inquiry of whether you called them. Anyone you actually did call who makes a rude return call can be zapped with a sweet "Why, hello there, how nice of you to call back; I was just trying to reach you."

A REPLY

DEAR MISS MANNERS—Please consider this factor in the Caller I.D. callbacks situation:

I have dialed a number, realized it was a wrong dialing and hung up. I have also unknowingly dialed wrong numbers. I have made a call for information and proceeded, after receiving no answer, to try another source. I made a call and, when there was no answer, took a nap.

In none of these instances did I want a return call. Please remind people to be extra polite when they make return calls that may be untimely or really not wanted.

GENTLE READER—Miss Manners has no trouble at all considering that the ability to dial back from a number that was called—by using Caller I.D. or dialing a telephone company code—should not be abused.

As a matter of fact, its best use is to deal with those who do abuse the telephone by making calls that are unpleasant or worse. It is handy to be able to trace such calls. Assuming that all aborted calls are such is to turn a nuisance tracker into a nuisance. This is not an advance in civilization.

THE TELEPHONE BILL

While Miss Manners puffs along as fast as she can to keep the rules updated to go with each new gadget, she is afraid that she may have been slipping behind in the matter of telephone bills.

The actual rule of etiquette has remained the same since the invention of the telephone: You do not stick anyone else with your telephone bills. Heretofore, developments in telephone billing procedures made this easier, not harder, to follow.

Before telephone credit cards became available, the choice for a guest was to leave the host embarrassingly trivial sums ascertained from an operator or to make all long-distance calls collect. In addition, it was necessary to apologize for any local calls that might add to the bill in areas where message units were charged.

That the owner of the telephone was supposed to say, "Oh, for heaven's sake, how much can it be—just go ahead and make the call and don't worry about it" did not relieve the caller from keeping anything more than a few pennies off the bill. As one cannot easily give (and even less easily accept) guest-to-host reimbursement, a polite houseguest with a lot of calls to make would have to claim other errands and get to a public telephone.

Now anyone with a card can charge it all and spare hosts this expense. The fastidious (and well-heeled) guest can also spare a host the necessity of answering the visitor's calls and having the house line tied up by bringing a telephone of his or her own.

So far, so good. But all of these ideas have been built on the assumptions that the telephone from which a call originates bears all the charges and the expense of making local calls is negligible.

With portable telephones of various kinds, the person who receives a call is probably being charged for air time. The charge for a local call from such a telephone is likely to be way beyond what would be dropped into a pay phone for the same call. So Miss Manners has had to develop two new rules:

1. When given the number of a portable telephone, one should inquire when it should be used.

Sample dialogue:

Q: "Is this for emergency use?"

A: "No, I'm on the road a lot; call me any time," or "Well, unless it's urgent, it might be better to try me at home first."

2. One must try to avoid using anyone else's portable telephone, to the extent of making at least a polite argument if it is offered.

Sample dialogue:

Q: "When you get a chance, would you mind pulling over to a gas station? I need to make a call."

A: "Okay." Or "Why don't you just use the car phone?"

Q: "Oh, no, thank you, I'll just use a pay phone."

A: "Don't be silly—I'd much rather you did than that we take the time to stop."

If the passenger doesn't acquiesce at this point, the driver may safely assume that the excuse of a call is a euphemism and should pull into a gas station as requested.

TELEPHONE PROCEDURE

SCREENING CALLS

Telephone tag is quickly becoming a major sport. Everybody is crying foul and nobody is getting through the lines. It is time for the etiquette umpire to step in.

Miss Manners trusts that everyone is familiar with the basic game of My Time Is More Important Than Your Time. It requires four players on two teams, each consisting of a "boss" and a "secretary."

The secretary of one team places a call to the secretary of the other, asking for that team's boss to be put on the line. The receiving secretary is then required to stall while suggesting that the initiating player first put that team's boss on the line. The team whose boss is on the line first loses, with extra points for the amount of time that boss stays on the line before the other boss gets on.

This is not an efficient, let alone pleasant, way to do business, as the moves and feints can go on while business empires fall. The enjoyment is supposed to be in the sport itself. Like sports requiring expensive horses or cars, as well as lots of idle time, it has hitherto been confined to the rich—in this case, the salaried, rather than the landed, rich—with nothing better to do. Thus it did little harm to the society at large.

Now answering machines and voice mail have made the sport available to the general population, both on the job and in their own homes. Many of those people do have useful things to do. A good number of them are getting frightfully annoyed at the waste of their time.

There has tended to be a lot of false blame placed. Screening calls is not itself rude. Miss Manners has a hard time trying to make the irate understand that. It was the people who originated telephone tag as a way of determining status who gave a bad name to the state of having anything else in the world to do besides take telephone calls—in other words, of having a life.

Even the wildly condemned practice of leaving a machine on at home so that one knows who is calling before deciding whether to answer is not rude. Some calls are more urgent than others, which is not to say that callers who may be looking for a chat may not be as, or more, lovable than those calling to say that one's house is on fire.

It is no more possible or wise always to accept all calls as they are made than it is to leave one's front door wide open. The blame for rudeness properly belongs to the person who makes a call without taking this into account, not the one who defers a call that comes in at the wrong time.

The machinery can even be used entirely for back-and-forth

messages, without necessitating that both people be available at once; to set up regular calling hours, at which one will be reachable; and to encourage people to write letters.

For those who need to talk, politeness requires that they recognize the necessity of negotiating a mutually convenient time. Being asked to leave a message is neither a rejection nor a disgrace. The message should include various suggested times for the return call, which also spares the caller the necessity of being constantly at liberty.

Business calls may properly be screened for content, so that they can be properly routed—provided that this does not require the caller to repeat the story more than once. Personal calls require only a name, because no one would call anyone at home who was not already an acquaintance (in Miss Manners' dreams).

But businesses that solicit or place calls ought to have people easily available at the convenience of those whom they wish to have call. Trying to capture people's attention requires making it convenient for them to choose the talking time and businesses that make their customers wait to be called back are violating that rule. In that case, it is the originator of the idea—please do business with us—who yields convenience to the customer. Otherwise, it is the person who originates the call itself who allows the person being called to set a time to talk.

So the very premise of Executive Telephone Tag was in error. The person of higher status is not, as those players imagine, the one who keeps other people waiting. It is the one who knows how to behave.

ROUTING CALLS

DEAR MISS MANNERS—At my office, everyone takes a turn filling in for the receptionist, which means a lunch hour of answering business calls from outside callers. A peculiar kind of caller believes that it is not necessary to identify himself or herself, but will demand this of others.

I will answer with "Good afternoon, XYZ Company," and the response is, "Who's this?"

Frankly, I am at a loss for a polite answer. A stunned "Excuse me?" doesn't work.

If I repeat the company name, they say, in a louder voice, "I said, 'Who is this?' "

I have tried "Who is calling, please?" or, when I am feeling literal, "This is the person you dialed, whom are you calling, please?" but the caller usually fails to grasp that they are being asked to comply with normal telephone protocol.

Clearly, these unidentified callers are demanding that I state MY name. I can only assume these people have some sad need to feel familiar with receptionists and are crudely noting a change from the usual voice.

I do not wish to give my name to an anonymous voice, especially on a phone line which is not my own. I do not believe my name is any of their concern—in such circumstances, my name is "the receptionist," and I would just like to put their call through.

Am I over-reacting by taking offense? Should I consider it part of the difficulty of dealing with the public? I guess I am looking for a way to keep my name to myself and not be fired in the process, as this kind of person can be quick to complain about not being treated "very friendly."

GENTLE READER—Miss Manners hardly knows whether she should exert herself to answer this question before the XYZ Company installs voice mail, which will render your problem moot. But as the theory behind voice mail is connected to your question, she will go ahead.

Your indignation is based on the erroneous assumption that the callers want to have a personal encounter with an individual when they telephone your company. People who call a business are much less likely to have an improper interest in the personalities they may encounter than a proper interest in knowing if they have the right functionary who will attend to their business.

The manners you cite apply to callers to a private household where it would be rude for the caller to ask the identity of the person answering the telephone and possibly dangerous for that person to reply.

In business, one gives one's name to callers who need it for legitimate business dealings. Such is not even the case in the calls you describe. Hearing a voice that is not that of the receptionist, they may well be inquiring whom they have reached out of fear that it is a wrong extension.

The proper reply for you to make is, indeed, that you are (temporarily) the receptionist, and would like to know, as voice mail will one day inquire, less individually but at least less grudgingly, where to send the call.

RETURNING CALLS

DEAR MISS MANNERS—While trying to contact people at work, I am often quizzed by the person answering the phone: Who are you, why do you want to speak with her, what company are you with, why can't you talk to me instead, etc.

I am sometimes sensitive about giving out information, in part because I am a therapist and am returning the call—information the inquisitive party need not know. Or perhaps it is a friend who has asked me to call and I am uncertain how their business policies about personal calls apply.

Do you have any suggestions about how to answer the twenty questions game with inquisitive third parties? Answers to their questions have little to do with my actually contacting the person I seek and are not passed on to that person. Usually, I state my preference of wanting to speak to that person in a pleasant, but firm, tone of voice.

GENTLE READER—Miss Manners is also uncertain about the policies about telephone calls at the particular businesses you happen to call, but she does not join you in considering them nosy to have any. The object is not to play games but to route the calls efficiently.

This is not to say that Miss Manners doesn't sympathize with the victims of abuse of such systems. To state that one is returning a call should be enough; anyone who persists in asking what it is about can fairly be told that that is exactly what you are hoping to find out by returning the call.

If you don't like calling your business "personal," you could call it "private." That way you make it clear that you must talk to the individual named while allowing the question to remain open of whether it is about medical problems or a corporate takeover.

IDENTIFYING CALLERS (BUSINESS)

DEAR MISS MANNERS—I have been answering phones in various offices for the last 14 years. When I hear "May I speak to Steve?" or "Steve, please," on a business call, I am always startled anew that the caller feels no need to identify himself when asking for the president of the company (or anyone, for that matter). I have to go through the rigamarole of questions every single time. Often the caller has called before.

Where did I go wrong, or what did I miss? No one ever says "This is John; may I please speak to Steve?" I don't know how much longer I can go on being polite in the face of this breach of the rules of etiquette, so important in keeping us civilized.

GENTLE READER—Miss Manners detects signs that you are already weakening under the strain. Otherwise, you would hardly let it pass without even a shudder that callers feel no need to identify the president of the company (or anyone else at the workplace) other than as "Steve." You would be within the bounds of courtesy to reply stiffly, "I beg your pardon? Are you referring to Mr. Whitherspoonfeld?"

But retraining your public is exactly what you are trying to avoid. Miss Manners can offer you no hope but lots of encouragement. Like you, she has been gently trying to prod people into learning and following and like you, she has noticed that some are slow learners. However, polite patience will eventually make a difference—she hopes.

IDENTIFYING CALLERS (PERSONAL)

DEAR MISS MANNERS—When I am calling a friend and her husband, whom I also know, answers, and I say, "Well, Frank, it's a nice day, may I speak to Lynn, please?" does he have the right to say "Who's calling?"

I am calling to speak to his wife, not to him and it annoys me. I feel as if I have to have his permission to complete my call. She is on my calling list for a group activity and I only state the time and date of the meeting; I do not gossip. How could I handle this?

GENTLE READER—Although Miss Manners approves of answering machines being used as home screening devices, she is not ordinarily crazy about family members who act as receptionists for one another.

It is too businesslike a procedure for home. After all, what are they going to say if your call is not welcome—"She's taking a meeting now"? There is nothing wrong with the blanket announcement to everyone that Lynn is not available at the moment, but that does not require the inquiry that annoys you.

That said, Miss Manners is going to align herself with Frank. When addressing a pleasantry to him, you are obliged to identify yourself. The poor soul has a right to know who has been telling him that it's a nice day.

THE WAKE-UP CALL

DEAR MISS MANNERS—I haven't seen you discuss the habit that some people have of calling up on the telephone and asking, "Did I wake you up?"

I think this is beastly rude, because they're inquiring into the other person's sleeping habits, which are none of their business, and also inquiring what the person was doing when they called, which is also none of their business.

I get the impression that they expect you to say "no," whether it's true or not. Instead, I always say "yes," whether it's true or not. I have an ex-friend who once replied to my "yes," with, "You're supposed to say no." That isn't the reason that she's an ex-friend, but I'm sure that there is a connection.

GENTLE READER—Now, just a minute here. Either you complain that this question is a serious, and therefore intolerable, inquiry into your personal habits, which you are obliged to answer honestly; or you have to acknowledge that it is a mere convention, to which a conventional rather than a literal answer is expected, in which case it is not nosy. You can't have it both ways.

The right way is to understand that it is a mere pleasantry, intended to mean, "I hope I didn't wake you up," and calls for polite reassurance. After all, the social lesson is probably already learned. It was the sleepiness in your voice that tipped off the caller to ask the question and should alert him or her not to call you at that time again.

You can politely temper that "no," even without resorting to the standard comical retort, "No, I had to get up anyway to answer the phone." You can say, "No, that's all right," which answers the implied apology, rather than the actual question. Slightly less charmingly, you can say, "I had to get up soon anyway." Or you can say, "That's okay, let me call you back later," and roll over and get back to sleep if you can.

THE DISCONNECTED CALL

DEAR MISS MANNERS—Who should take the initiative to call the other party after a disconnection? Should both parties continue to dial the other at the same time, or should one person assume the responsibility?

A mutual friend set me up on a blind date with her friend. She knows him both socially and professionally. This gentleman and I had an initial phone conversation and the following week we spoke again. During our second conversation, we were disconnected. Because I did not know who should accept responsibility for this error, I was unsure which individual should be obligated to call the other party back. After waiting a minute for him to call me, I decided to call and made a connection.

GENTLE READER—You were lucky you ever talked to this gentleman again. The standard procedure is that both people wait a minute for the other to call back and then dial each other at once and get busy signals.

This, as you shrewdly guessed, is why we have rules of etiquette. Unfortunately, however, we have two such rules:

1. The person who initiated the call should be the one to call back.

2. The person responsible for disconnecting should call back.

NOT RETURNING CALLS

DEAR MISS MANNERS—My boss seldom returns phone calls and when he does, it isn't promptly. I can't tell you how much abuse I am subjected to because of his lack of concern for others. When he does return a call, he tells the party that he has tried numerous times and the line was busy, or that no one answered. (These are all businesses with full-time personnel.) He also tells them he never got their messages.

How can I respond to "Did he get my messages?" or "Didn't you give him my message?" So far, I have politely replied that he gets all messages, but this doesn't convince many callers and I am further queried as to when did he get the message and why hasn't he returned the calls. After years of dealing with him, why haven't these callers learned that he isn't going to return their calls promptly, if at all?

GENTLE READER—Presumably, he or his business has compensating qualities. Otherwise, after years of dealing with him, you would have learned not to let him get away with involving you in his excuses.

Nevertheless, now would be a good time to stop. Aware of the constraints on criticizing a boss (on top of the universal requirement of doing everything to everyone politely), Miss Manners will suggest a particularly tactful way.

"It's not a good idea for you to claim you never got people's telephone messages," you might say in a good-natured tone that seems to regard his habit as charming naughtiness. "People are divided between thinking that you're lying or that I am—neither of which does much for the reputation of this office. Why don't I just warn people that you'd rather handle business by mail?"

Of course, Miss Manners has no idea whether your boss answers his mail, either. She's just assuming that he does *something* in order to stay in business.

ENDING THE CALL

"Well, I guess I'd better let you go now."

Miss Manners is not sure where this expression suddenly originated, but it has now spread everywhere, as the sign-off sentence for every telephone call. It means "I want to get off the phone. Now."

The correct reply is definitely not "Oh, that's okay, I have nothing special to do for a while, anyway, and I'd just as soon keep chatting." Rather, it is something along the lines of "Well, good to talk to you," which can be immediately followed by a crisp exchange of cordial good-byes. Thus, it is only a few graceful seconds from the offer to let the other person go and the release of the person who made the offer.

Miss Manners approves. We can't all hang on the telephone forever, but some people give it a try. They must be politely disentangled from other people's ears. It is no insult. Even the most fascinating of conversations must come to a close sometime and many polite people are reluctant to mutter, "I've got to go now," lest it sound too eager.

The suggestion that it is the other person's valuable time that must be respected, rather than one's own, is a triumph of etiquette. It reminds Miss Manners of an old gimmick that used to be suggested to the electronically desperate: Hang up in mid-sentence, but not on the other person, as that would be unspeakably rude. Hang up on yourself, instead, while you are talking enthusiastically. The person you hung up on is bound to think it is an accident.

Sure, but then that person would call back and say, "We were cut off." The new version is a marked improvement and, besides, it can be used more than once on the same person. It is also definitely better than the previous convention, which was "Wait a minute, I think I hear my mother calling me." Even if one presumes that Mother isn't announcing dinner from the kitchen, but rattling Call Waiting from her office, that one is a bit of a stretch to those of a certain age.

"I won't keep you" is wonderful. But in a way, Miss Manners hates to draw attention to it because such usage is in bad repute nowadays, when so many people think they want the direct and unvarnished literal truth.

On the contrary, conventions are what we need to prevent us from telling one another such unbearable truths as "Look, you've told me this story seven times before and I find myself siding with everyone who you say is against you, and I've got better things to do now, such as talk to my plants." The fact is that we have always had to use less than literal conventions in order to be able to part from any encounter with anyone. No polite person wants to say outright, "This has been great, but enough is enough."

CALL AVOIDING

We have eliminated the telephone from modern life. Have you noticed?

Perhaps not. There are all those instruments around, not only on walls and tables, but being snappily unfolded from briefcases and pockets. People seem to be talking on them.

Don't be fooled. Nobody is actually reaching anyone else on the telephone. They are all just trying to find out when other people might be available, in offices as well as homes. What used to be telephones are now just elaborate message-exchanging devices.

Miss Manners is not complaining. On the contrary: She feels vindicated. All these years—roughly from the time dear Mr. Bell explained the thing to her and she stopped cupping her ear and saying, "What?"—Miss Manners has been pointing out the flaw in the concept of the telephone.

The flaw is that while everybody would like to be able to have instant access to everybody else, nobody wants to live on constant alert. Miss Manners is used to such contradictions. Her whole field of etiquette is one that nobody wants to practice, but everybody wants others to practice.

Nevertheless, Miss Manners admits that she is puzzled about why people go to such trouble and expense to purchase the equipment with which to enable others to reach them at all times and places. Do they like being interrupted in the middle of breakthrough ideas, vacations, strategy sessions, baths, drives, romances or any combination of these?

Well, no. This is why they also buy answering machines, install voice mail and attach gadgets that enable them to tell who is calling so that they do not have to answer the telephone. And if someone does manage to catch them, they now have that vile Call Waiting as an escape.

Now that everybody has all that stuff, we have reached an impasse. When it is all working properly, people who make telephone calls reach only recorded messages and recording devices; those who call them back encounter the same treatment. We are just where we would have been if nobody had a telephone.

Miss Manners is not convinced that people really understand how much telephone privacy good manners actually entitles them to have. The fact is that etiquette simply does not require you to take any telephone call that happens to come in, any more than it requires you to allow the whole world to drop in at your house or office.

Somehow, popular belief has turned this topsy-turvy. People who do not get on the telephone every time it rings are the ones who are being accused of bad manners, not those who demand that they do so.

Miss Manners is aware that methods of screening calls can themselves be rude. The person who keeps saying "Who?" instead of listening to the name, and the answering machine that drones on with its dreary little jokes, are a nuisance. But it is not unreasonable to reschedule or reroute telephone calls. These are appointments, and should be given their proper time, agreeable and convenient to both parties. Then they can be given both parties' full attention. No one will need to drop an actual visitor in order to take an electronic one and, best of all, no one will need Call Waiting, which Miss Manners has no ambiguity about at all. She loathes it.

UNLISTED NUMBERS

It seems that telephone books are shrinking. As ever more people request that their numbers be unlisted, it is going to be increasingly hard for small children to reach their dinner plates. This troubles Miss Manners, who would hate to see parents having to choose between refining the intellect and refining the table manners, depending on to which use they put the encyclopedia.

The usual analysis of people who don't want to be reached day or night by whoever is leafing through the telephone book is that they must be dreadful snobs. (That there might be something arrogant in expecting to be able to reach anyone at any time is not considered.) An updated version of this is the declaration that Californians, for having a statewide high proportion of unlisted numbers, are demonstrably "self-absorbed," which is rather a severe name for having other things to do.

Miss Manners would like to suggest that a few telephone manners might help alleviate the situation.

The worst offenders, everyone seems to agree, are businesses that solicit business by telephone. Even the unlisted number is not a protection against this invasion when numbers are dialed randomly. Answering machines may intercept such calls, but can become tied up in doing so.

Unfortunately, etiquette can only appeal to people's better nature to make them behave better, which is not a notably successful technique when dealing with commercial interests. But Miss Manners would like to point out to the recipients of unwanted calls that there is nothing rude about refusing to cooperate. At the first sign that it is not a personal call, one may say, "I'm sorry, I'm not interested" and hang up. When the technique of invading households is no longer effective, it will be dropped.

It is not rude to make calling hours known to acquaintances—"It's best to reach me early in the morning"; "We eat at seven, and don't take calls until nine to about ten-thirty"; "I don't answer the telephone before noon." Callers should inquire if it is "a good time to talk" and those called may say, without having to offer excuses, "No—could I call you back in about an hour?"

Just these simple rules would ease the burden, perhaps even to the point where we would not have to hide out from one another just to be free from interruption.

Of course, one may ask why people who are troubled by calls have telephones at all. Why, to call other people, of course—and get all upset if they refuse to answer.

THE UNWANTED CALL (PART ONE)

DEAR MISS MANNERS—When dealing with telephone solicitors for charities, when one is not interested or able to contribute to their cause, I believe the courteous method is to allow the representative to explain the cause fully, ask for a contribution and then politely say that I am unable to help at this time. My friend thinks I am wasting the charity's time, as well as mine, and should immediately interject and say I am not interested. Please inform as to the proper method.

GENTLE READER—Having so often opposed telephone solicitors who are (as they are quick to point out) only trying to earn a living or help a good cause, Miss Manners is reluctant to discourage any courtesy that may come their way.

Certainly, she has never condoned rudeness toward them. All she has done is to point out that their job requires them to intrude upon people's lives and that people who do not want to listen to their pitches are justified in cutting them short by saying, "Thank you, but I'm not interested," and terminating the call.

Now here you are, not interested, but willing to listen. This is kindly meant and if your mind is not totally made up about the charity in question, it is a good idea. But Miss Manners cannot think that you are doing the callers a favor to prolong the conversation when you are determined not to make a donation and they could be talking to someone who might be persuaded to do so.

THE UNWANTED CALL (PART TWO)

DEAR MISS MANNERS—I keep getting calls from brokers and other salesmen trying to sell hot stocks, limited partnerships and various other investments. I try to end these conversations in a polite way, but lately have found myself just hanging up without explanation, especially when unable to squeeze in a "not interested" comment. Is it rude to hang up the phone in such circumstances?

GENTLE READER—Miss Manners is obliged to tell you that yes, it is rude to hang up on a human being without offering any explanation. But you will find her considerably more lenient if we discuss those circumstances.

By your own account, you have tried explaining that you are not interested in the proposition being described; you abandoned this attempt because you were unable to "squeeze in" your statement. Try again. Start with a quick "Excuse me!" in the hope that the caller will pause to hear your statement, which, after all, kindly saves that person from wasting time.

If there is no reaction to your interjection, Miss Manners gives you full permission to conclude that what you have there is not, after all, a human being, capable of listening, but an automated device that can neither respond to others nor harbor hurt feelings if halted. So hang up.

CHAPTER 4

THE RECORDED WORD

PLUS ÇA CHANGE . . .

In an era long ago, some of the most frequently asked—no, sputtered—etiquette questions concerned telephone answering machines.

"How dare they screen their calls?" was one. "I'm sure they were home and they just didn't pick up the phone. They were probably sitting there listening to me say my name and deciding they didn't want to talk to me. Don't you think it's rude to pick and choose whose calls you'll take and whose not?"

Another was "Don't you think it's rude when people expect me to talk to their stupid machines? Either they're there, or they're not. What has happened to the human touch?"

Miss Manners offered no comfort to people who resisted this useful device. The most she would do was to attempt to protect them from the tedious recordings to which people used to subject their callers back when the answering machine was a novelty.

(The only genuine humor in those days came from earnest but pathetic attempts to issue instructions: "Don't record until you hear—well, it's not exactly a beep, but more of a whistle and after that you have ten seconds, maybe twenty, but anyway not more, to leave your message, but don't forget to leave your name and when you called—oh, and the date—and we'll try to get back to you as soon as we can, but we might be away, or you can try us at work, or maybe you better leave a message there anyway, in case this thing isn't working, because we've been having trouble with it.")

The argument about favoring human beings over machinery didn't have its usual stunning effect on Miss Manners, because she didn't consider it applicable. She saw it as a matter of pitting one machine—the telephone, with its arrogant habit of demanding immediate attention no matter what it might be interrupting—against a machine designed to tame its tyranny, and she sided with the latter.

Nor was she willing to anthropomorphize the machines. Machines are not people. There's a big difference between cursing a coffee machine and cursing a waiter; or between kicking automobile tires and kicking automobile mechanics.

When Miss Manners tries to get this point across, she encounters resistance from people who declare, for example, "Hanging up on my answering machine is like hanging up on me." No, it's not. You have to make that vital distinction between leaving polite messages, because they are directed at the person who collects the messages, and trying to exchange pleasantries with a recorded voice.

It was a big relief when people stopped all that fuss because they got used to answering machines. Unfortunately, the relief didn't last. In came the second wave of sputtering about answering machines:

"I had to call and call and call, and there was no way to leave a message. Do they think I have nothing better to do with my time? Don't you think it's rude of people not to have answering machines?"

"Somebody else answered the phone, and I had to get involved talking to some stranger who wanted to know who I was and probably never even bothered to pass on my message. Isn't it rude not to make it easy for people to leave messages?"

Miss Manners wouldn't swear that the very same people who used to raise the humanity argument against voice mail are the ones who now complain that they are kept waiting forever for a simple answer because they are forced to wait for a person. But the irritation level sounds familiar.

The absence of a car telephone or a cellular telephone further infuriates determined callers. What do people mean by telling them later that they didn't get on the line because they were "out"? What kind of an excuse is that?

Lately, Miss Manners has noticed, relentless communicators have stopped asking others, "Do you have a fax?" They now ask, "What's your fax number?" If the first question is answered anyway, rather than the second, and in the negative, they turn frostily incredulous. "You don't have a fax? How do people reach you?"

On E-mail, of course. What, you don't have an E-mail address? How do you expect . . .

Never mind. The etiquette rule that covers all of this unseemly talk is that it is rude to bully people whom you hope to reach because they do not provide the technology that would enable you to make them stop whatever else they may be doing and attend to you immediately.

It is not rude not to hold yourself constantly on call by any or all means. It is all right to be busy, to be out, or to be otherwise unavailable—provided you don't force other people to listen to a recorded comic account of why you are unavailable.

USING THE MACHINE

DEAR MISS MANNERS—A couple who are friends of ours have a policy of never answering their telephone; every call goes through their answering machine. Later, sometimes two days later, they return your call. Keep in mind, this couple has no children, the wife works part time on occasion and no other activity in their home.

I object to having every call screened and I think it is inconsiderate. Sometimes you only need a short answer to a question such as, "What time do we meet before the movie?" It appears to me that they are accumulating information and responding after all the offers are received, then tailoring their replies based on the last phone call. Am I wrong to think that screening 100% of your phone calls for two years is abominable behavior?

GENTLE READER—Don't you suppose that these people might object to having their lives screened?

For their own decision on whether to admit visitors to their own home, you have scrutinized their family structure and professional and personal activities and decided that they have unjustified and socially sneaky motives. Miss Manners is not surprised that they are not so eager to hear from you as to be willing to allow you to dictate the terms.

It's kind of too bad. Theirs sounds like such a pleasant home, where an invited guest would receive uninterrupted attention in a peaceful atmosphere.

Miss Manners would have been more sympathetic had you complained that their habit had actually caused you a reasonable inconvenience. A legitimate complaint, such as "I thought we were supposed to meet at the movies, but we never agreed on a time, and when you didn't respond to my inquiry, I was forced to get there an hour early for fear of missing you," is one in which she would support you.

ABUSING THE MACHINE

DEAR MISS MANNERS—Three times during the past year, I received news of a friend's death on my telephone answering machine. To hear of a beloved one's passing is, of course, always saddening, but to get this shock from an unresponsive machine with which one can share no expression of grief adds, I believe, a grimness and a coldness that should—and could—be avoided.

Granted that in two of my three cases, the caller directly apologized for conveying this news by machine, I feel strongly that a message telling me to return the call on account of "urgent" or "tragic" news would not only better prepare me (or anyone) but also would help open the communication of feelings that the ancient rituals of grieving properly include. It is far better to hear sad tidings from a live consoling friend than from an impersonal unresponsive machine. So I am asking Miss Manners to lay down the proper etiquette for using the new technology to convey messages concerning a loved one's death.

GENTLE READER—Although Miss Manners agrees that this machine has no role in transmitting such tragic news, she knows how frustrating it can be to be kept from getting through with such urgent information. The people who called you probably had many such calls to make under the pressure of letting people know of the death in time to attend the funeral. At least they recognized the obligation to inform relatives and close friends.

The difficulty is to leave a message that will ensure a prompt return call without issuing a general alarm, such as "I have something terrible to tell you," that could cause widespread panic. One might say, "Please call me immediately—it's important," with an injunction to keep trying if the caller is likely to be tying up the number left.

Miss Manners only hopes that all of the people involved had already obeyed her rule against silly recorded messages. Persisting in calling someone under these circumstances and being forced to listen over and over to a humorous routine while waiting to announce a death is well nigh unbearable.

BUSINESS ANSWERING MACHINES

DEAR MISS MANNERS—I'd like to know how Miss Manners feels about the increasing use of telephone answering machines by individuals working within large organizations. These machines are used on their business extensions.

Surely any office with more than five persons can afford to have someone man the phones at all times, especially during business hours. To make matters worse, these individuals don't even return your call when you leave a message.

GENTLE READER—Miss Manners suspects that people always expect her to side against any machine, no matter how useful a function it may be serving. Why is that? Do they believe there is a backward time capsule hidden in her chignon?

It strikes her that simple message taking is something that machines do extremely well, especially compared to some people she has encountered. She would not be so nosy as to suggest what others can or cannot afford, but the answering machine seems preferable to the overworked operator who must chew lunch while answering telephones and resort to the Hold button or other forms of electronic torture.

This is not to suggest that Miss Manners believes machines can replace human beings in more complex tasks. One of them is returning telephone calls. Miss Manners feels you have blamed the machine system unjustly for failure to return your calls. It was not required to do so. It already had its conversation with you.

THE MACHINE'S MESSAGE

DEAR MISS MANNERS—On a home answering machine, is it necessary to include an apology? For example, would it be acceptable to say, "Hello. We are unable to answer the phone at this time; however, you may wish to leave a message"?

For office use, must one do anything other than state one's name and indicate a message may be left? E.g., "This is ————. Please leave a message."

Now that most people are familiar with these devices, it would seem polite to subject the caller to as brief a message as possible. (We will not again discuss the indignities involved in having to wait through a message that not only is long, but also an ill-fated attempt at humor.)

GENTLE READER—Miss Manners is all for telephone brevity, especially at the expense of wit. How grateful she is that you understand that answering machines should never be used to audition vaudeville acts.

It is true that everyone now knows to wait for the beep before attempting to leave a message on a machine. So let us agree that the instructions may be omitted. But Miss Manners does not grudge the two seconds it takes to be polite. A simple "We are sorry" before the part about not being able to answer the telephone now doesn't take all that long.

Note that this is coming from someone who has just been telling you that there is nothing impolite about not taking calls. Nevertheless, one should be delicately regretful that anyone else was inconvenienced by one's own—legitimate—convenience.

THE WRONG ANSWERING MACHINE

DEAR MISS MANNERS—Like many people now, I have an answering machine on my telephone. My recorded message states: "You have reached [telephone number], and, as usual, I can't come to the phone right now. Please leave your name, phone number and a convenient time to call, and I'll get back to you. Thank you."

Frequently, I'll get recorded messages that are obviously for another phone number. Am I obligated to return these calls and inform the callers that they reached the wrong party? I believe that if they were irresponsible (clumsy, dumb) enough to dial a wrong number, I am being put upon to return the calls and inform them of this.

One woman has called several times and leaves a message for "John" to call her. I am not John, but I don't want to be bothered with her calling again. These wrong numbers are an inconvenience to me and having to call them back is a further imposition. What is the correct thing to do?

GENTLE READER—Miss Manners doesn't suppose you would like to hear the kind thing to do, would you?

This would be to be slightly more tolerant of the errors of others. The reason you haven't heard from some of your own treasured chums for a while now is that the people on whose answering machines they left you messages decided they were too clumsy and dumb to be worth helping.

Besides, it seems to Miss Manners that John's friend is inconveniencing you ever so much more by continuing to call than if you made only one call to set her straight. How can you bear to think of her languishing away from what she believes to be John's inconstant heart when such a simple gesture might smooth their way? If they decided to live happily ever after, they wouldn't need to dial each other and your problem would be solved.

CHAPTER 5

THE WRITTEN WORD

FORM

OBSERVING THE FORMS

Let others bemoan the demise of the art of letter writing. Miss Manners despairs of ever again seeing a letter that is just properly addressed.

Forms for writing the name, date, salutation and closing for a social or business letter are really quite simple. It takes about thirty seconds to memorize them, and they can pretty much be used forever, without having to think about them again. But thinking about them is exactly what people have been doing, more's the pity. So an easy task was made difficult by everyone's feeling obliged to invent his or her own system.

Miss Manners can't understand why people don't want to save time and effort by adopting standard procedures for so mundane a task. Must you really apply all your creativity to the address? No wonder there's none left for the body of the letter and preprinted cards have to be found even for such elementary messages as "Thinking of you" and "Please come to dinner."

Risk is also involved when you make up your own forms of address. These may be deconstructed by a recipient who decides that you have slyly inserted an offensive meaning. Or they may be scandalously sloppy, to the point of insult.

Insulting someone simply by the way in which you address the envelope strikes Miss Manners as rather a shame. The victim may be too angry to open the letter, in which you could really deliver an original insult, if that is your inclination.

Admittedly, people are also now given to inventing idiosyncratic forms by which they expect to be addressed, and the innocent letter writer may ignite wrath simply by guessing wrong. Therefore many of them trim the addresses of everything they can, in the hopes of omitting whatever may be offensive. But those very omissions make the letter offensively curt.

Here are the standard forms, with some of the standard variations. If you get into trouble using them, Miss Manners promises to defend you.

You must begin by putting a person's correct name on the envelope. This may sound obvious, but even formal invitations are routinely addressed nowadays with nicknames, misspellings and such anonymous descriptions as "and family," ". . . guest," ". . . escort," or ". . . children."

Miss Manners is sorry if it is too much trouble to find out the actual names of the people you care enough about to invite to a formal occasion, but you must do it. If a guest is to be permitted to bring someone else along, you must find out the name of that person and put it on the invitation. People resident in the same household may be addressed on the same invitation, but each must be named.

All names on envelopes must carry honorifics. The bald name with no title is rude. Ah, you say, but which title? Whatever you pick—Mr., Ms., Mrs., Miss, Dr., Serene Highness—it turns out that the person is indignantly expecting to be called something else.

If you know what your correspondent prefers, you use it, even if you personally believe that any lady who calls herself Mrs. is shaming her own identity, or that any married lady who doesn't is dishonoring her own husband. For those whose preferences are not known, Miss Manners uses Ms. for ladies younger than she and Miss or Mrs. for those her age or older, hoping that anyone whom she would honor with a letter would have too much sense to pick a fight. Two lines of address are used for couples who do not go by "Mr. and Mrs."—the lady first, with her title and name, and the gentleman second, with his. Small children are given the thrill of seeing themselves grandly addressed as Miss or Master.

On a business letter, it is entirely possible that you may not know the name or gender of the person who will handle the letter. In that case, the salutation is "Ladies and Gentlemen:" or "Dear Madam or Sir." When a name is known, the person is addressed as "Dear Ms." or "Mr." with the surname. The would-be friends-of-all-the-world would be surprised to know how offended many people are when strangers or business acquaintances assume use of their first names.

Such a letter carries the date on the upper right side, the writer's address either centered on the page or after a space and below the date and the name and address of the recipient next, on the left side of the page. Social letters may have a full date or just the day of the week (which annoys people who save love letters, but is not incorrect) and may omit the recipient's full name and address.

Conventional salutations and closings may not be omitted, even if you don't think they accurately describe the state in which you offer yourself. Business letters are signed "Yours truly"; those for whom that is not passionate enough may use "Very truly yours." In social letters "sincerely" is substituted for "truly" (oh, don't ask Miss Manners why; this is just custom) but could warm right up to "Affectionately" or "Love and kisses"—at which point Miss Manners has stopped reading over your shoulder, anyway.

ESCHEWING THE FORMS

MISS MANNERS—My long practice on business letters has been to omit the greeting entirely, and start out at once with what I have to say, as I have done with this letter. The letter title block, including the address, functions as a greeting, so an additional greeting serves no purpose.

I have never had anyone object. Nor has anyone ever complained because I omit a "complimentary close" and merely sign my name right after my message ends. French language letters make such a big thing of greetings and closings that they run about one-quarter longer than English language letters. Invariably such canned phrases are simply ignored.

GENTLE READER—Really? Miss Manners will have to tell her old friend Germaine de Staël that she has been wasting her time. You're not wasting any time on courtesy, are you?

You are, however, wasting your time if you are waiting for Miss Manners to congratulate you on your attempt to stamp out the pitifully few courtesies we have left.

Why bother with salutations and closings? Why bother saying "Good morning" or "Good-bye" when you can simply start barking at people, or turn on your heel and leave them? Because the abruptness is unpleasant, and softening it is a very easy way to demonstrate goodwill.

Now Miss Manners will wish you a good day. Those versed in the conventions will recognize this particular form as the courteous way of saying, "We seem to have nothing more to say to each other."

WRITING PAPER

DEAR MISS MANNERS—Is ecru-white writing paper an acceptable substitute for plain white in all cases? I have invested in both unengraved and engraved letter sheets, notes and calling cards, all engraved in black on ecru paper or card stock. I also plan to add engraved correspondence cards and informals at a later date.

I don't send many flowers, but I have found the cards to be useful as wedding gift enclosures. People do seem to get married quite often these days. Naturally, I use white lettersheets for condolence letters, but is ecru inappropriate?

I had read that both white and ecru were considered formal and equally serious when engraved with black ink, but you stated that you use cream (?) lettersheets engraved in brown for frivolous letters. Oh, dear, I'm not a very frivolous person at all. Must I re-order in white at once?

GENTLE READER—Indeed, people do seem to be getting married quite often these days. Why do you suppose that is?

Oops, there was Miss Manners drifting off frivolously again. Time to get out the brown ink. It is the brown engraving, not the ecru or cream (at least she didn't call it "creme," as the cosmetics companies do—oops) paper that makes Miss Manners' informal paper frivolous.

CUTE WRITING PAPER

DEAR MISS MANNERS—I understand why business letters and thank you letters must be written on white writing paper, but is it improper to write a personal letter on "cute" stationery? I have several different kinds of paper and write a countless number of personal letters each week.

GENTLE READER—Writing personal letters to people who have the same sense of cute as you do is exactly the purpose for which cute writing paper was invented—that and doing shopping lists on the back of it.

Just make sure the cuteness isn't in conflict with the body of the letter. Miss Manners recently received a very gracious note that a Gentle Reader had written on yellow paper on the top of each page of which was printed, "I'm mad as hell, and I'm not going to take it anymore!" This left her puzzled. She thought that "any more" required two words.

BUSINESS WRITING PAPER

DEAR MISS MANNERS—Imagine my dismay upon receiving a reply to a personal invitation on the embossed letterhead of the respondent's legal firm. The occasion was my nephew's graduation party and the invitation was mailed to a longtime family friend with whom we have no professional bonds.

While speculating upon the etiquette of sending regrets to a social occasion through the channels of one's typist, my sister informed me that perhaps this is proper behavior for a gentleman of his "profession." To assuage the current tension arising from this latent burst of sibling disagreement, as well as from the thinly disguised curl of disapproval now distorting my lips, I would appreciate your opinion.

GENTLE READER—This is the kind of letter, both for its point of view and its style, that Miss Manners is likely to be unjustly accused of making up. Perhaps she will ask you for the name of this lawyer, in case she needs to squelch such slander.

She knows that this lawyer is on duty all the time, from his apparent failure to understand that there is any such thing as private life. Perhaps it could be explained to him as that part of life which is unbillable. Although the misuse of office writing paper for private purposes is common among lawyers, it is inexcusable. Other professions go in for this travesty also, but it is particularly unpleasant to make an innocent person, who wants only to enjoy the company of an old friend, have that heart-stopping moment of seeing a law firm return address in the mail and wondering who was suing now.

COUPLES' WRITING PAPER

Why Miss Manners has a soft spot for curmudgeons, she is not sure. It couldn't be that she, the sweet voice of reason, resembles one herself. They are all bristling with indignation and she is in the business of calming people down.

It is probably something about the way curmudgeons go about expressing their wonder that the world is never up to standard. Miss Manners is so used to complaints being blurted with staggering bluntness that she appreciates people who take the trouble to express their irascibility at length. They are so deliciously astounded, outraged and floored by irony that they conjure up a world in which everything normally functions—well, normally.

Every curmudgeon worthy of the name suggests that each new complaint is felt so strongly because it represents an unprecedented low. Miss Manners finds this reassuring. She was thus receptive to a gentleman who requested the proper form of letterhead for the paper on which to write such missives. He plans to write letters to editors, to Congress, and other such standing targets, in his own name and his wife's, expressing, as that lady put it, "criticism, outrage, amusement, incredulity or even approval."

As the gentleman in question is a doctor and his wife is a lawyer, he set out six choices for Miss Manners, which combine various versions of their names, nicknames, initials, honorifics and titles, from "Dr. and Mrs." ("we find this archaic for other than formal, social correspondence but recognize its conservative appearance may help certain messages") to successive listings with a rat-a-tat-tat of degrees.

Miss Manners took the sixth choice, which was "other." A marriage, not being a corporation, issues only social communications. Therefore, there is no proper corporate letterhead for husband and wife, not even that intimidatingly conservative "Dr. and Mrs." The double name (together or in two-line listings, lady first, for couples who have different surnames), is only proper when used on cards. Two people can issue an invitation on a large card and send a present with a small card, but only one person can write a letter. Even firms with partners' names running up, down and sideways have only one person sign a letter that speaks on the firm's behalf.

This is something newly married couples have a hard time with, used as they are to tossing in each other's names. It saddens Miss Manners that well-meaning ones spend good money on paper improperly marked with both their names, ordered for letters thanking guests who send wedding presents. The thanking must be done, and it must be done in both names, but it must be written by only one person using his own paper—or hers, as the case may be. Miss Manners doesn't much care which person writes the letter, as long as only one person signs it. The other is included by such a phrase as "My husband and I were shocked by your vote on the budget."

Such are the rules. But Miss Manners mentioned that she has a soft spot for curmudgeons and she has been able to come up with a loophole for them. That is that manifestos, even small ones such as letters to the editor, may traditionally contain more than one signature—"we the undersigned" sort of thing.

Therefore, without compromising her own professional ethics, Miss Manners could allow these people to create paper with both their names, if they promised to use it only for such letters and not socially. In keeping with professional practice, she would suggest that they set out both their full names separately, without the honorifics that are used socially, but also without their professional degrees unless these are relevant to the issue discussed in the letter. She could allow all this, but she won't. She would be doing them no favor.

First, since the form would be newly minted, it would tip off an astute editor or member of Congress (and Miss Manners has known one or two of each) that the writers were regulars. "Oh, here is the Crank family checking in again" would be the response.

Second, it is bound to cause family friction. The most obliging spouse in the world doesn't sign onto every curmudgeonly opinion, and authorization must be obtained for each one. A truly obliging spouse will protect the curmudgeon with an occasional "Yes, dear, but I think it might be imprudent to send this one, at least until you've copied it over without the splotches on the page."

The gentleman would be best off signing his own name and allowing the wife to add hers as she sees fit. If he really can't control himself, he can write for himself alone, adding, "My wife is a lawyer and if you don't do what I say, she is going to beat you up."

THE INFORMAL

Although she generally does not care to associate with adjectives who arrive unaccompanied by nouns, Miss Manners would like to put in a good word for the informal.

Standing rather foolishly alone, an informal is not an attitude, but a piece of paper with one's name or monogram on it. It is such a dear, useful thing that she has forgiven its grammatical confusion. "I'm going to save you having to bother much by making your minimum efforts look wonderful," it promises. "You won't even have to exhaust yourself, poor thing, by writing your name."

The old informal was a folded card ("informal" being its nickname, in keeping with the spirit of the thing) about four inches wide and three inches high. On the outside, it being folded across the top, it had a lady's name with honorific: "Mrs.

Eugene Randolph Sniggle." Gentlemen did not use foldover cards alone, but there were "Mr. and Mrs." versions with a one-line address (everybody knew what city you lived in and the world was not yet divided by Zip) in the lower right corner.

One wrote breathless little messages on page three. But for those who didn't run out of breath in time, there was a dilemma about where to continue. Most people settled for page two, which put the bottom half of the message above its top half when the card was spread out. Life used to be full of these little puzzles.

As post office regulations became more stringent, the informal characteristically became more flexible. Gracefully, it unfolded itself and grew a half to three-quarters of an inch in both directions. The flat informal had the name centered at the top, perhaps with an address in the upper right-hand corner. Gentlemen could have them, too.

You would think it would be obvious that an informal was never intended to serve for formal invitations or formal letters, but its most constant misuse is by inexperienced brides (starting back when there was such a thing as an inexperienced bride) to write letters thanking people for wedding presents.

But for true informality—invitations and responses to such relaxed gatherings as tea, or sweet comments on charming occasions—it is perfect. So much better than voice mail.

Salutations and signatures are not required. The sender's name is right there. For notes, one puts a modest pen slash through the honorific; or a lady who uses her husband's full name may slash him out entirely (well, no; only on the informal) and sign herself with initials.

It is a tremendous advantage, in this period of choice, to be able to tell people how one wishes to be addressed in return. Mrs. Sniggle now hates being called that, for reasons only partly related to Mr. Sniggle, and has had her informals redone as "Ms. Angel Rocker-Sniggle."

The exertion of writing a full sentence is not even required. This is a place for what used to be carelessly chic (and economical) telegraph style: "Tea, Thursday the 8th, at four"; "Loved seeing you"; "Arriving Sunday"; "Be out of town Sunday—hate to miss you."

Informals can be sent with presents, instead of the smaller card; as an ultra-chic postcard in an envelope; and in place of greeting cards, where a minimal greeting ("Congratulations," "Happy birthday," "I'm crazy about you") carries more social weight than any printed matter.

OLD WRITING PAPER

DEAR MISS MANNERS—I'm an aspiring comedian and writer and a few years ago I invested in a logo design and business stationery, as I wanted to seem as professional as possible when I sent out headshots and material, even if my office was also my bedroom. Since then, I've had to move.

Is there an acceptable way to cross out the old address and write in a new one? Or is this so gauche that I should use plain paper until I get rich and/or sign a very long lease? My stash includes envelopes, business sized sheets, mailing labels and business cards.

GENTLE READER—People believe that etiquette conspires with the silver, catering and other luxury industries to make honest people spend more than they can afford, don't they? That Miss Manners would therefore probably denounce any economy as rude, maybe just to be mean and maybe to collect a kickback.

Well, much as she hates to disillusion everyone, the fact is that etiquette tends to shy away from extravagance. She sees nothing at all wrong in crossing out an old address and writing in a new one, as a sensible way of avoiding waste.

SALUTATIONS TO THOSE OF UNKNOWN GENDER

DEAR MISS MANNERS—The use of "To Whom It May Concern" in business correspondence is just plain gauche. In these times, the greetings "Dear Sir" or "Gentlemen" may offend your unknown audience immediately.

I consider "Gentlemen, Ladies," a respectful salutation, but I'm not sure it shows a proper business formality. Conversely, "Gentlemen, Mesdames" is formal, but foreign for English usage. Does the rule "Ladies first" apply? Who should be addressed first?

Some have suggested a simple, straightforward "Hello" as suitable to these relaxed times. And what about "Ms."? If you were a well ranked business executive, how would you prefer to be addressed by writers?

GENTLE READER—"Madam" will do just fine and, since you are writing, you don't need to bow. With a lady's surname, "Ms." is the correct business form, unless you happen to know that she prefers "Miss" or "Mrs."

Miss Manners begs you to stop working on these matters before you decide that the correct business salutation should be "Hey, Guys—How ya doin'?" and the closing, "Well, gotta go now." The correct singular address when the gender is unknown is "Dear Madam or Sir," and the plural, "Ladies and Gentlemen:"—both nice, simple, conventional phrases, with the lady's designation coming first simply because that is the way we are all used to hearing these phrases. In etiquette, she begs you to remember, originality doesn't count.

SALUTATIONS TO LADIES

DEAR MISS MANNERS—I have written a letter to an association dedicated to giving assertiveness lessons. Giving up on "Dear

Ladies" and "Mesdames," and unable to pluralize "Ms.," I called a friend for help. The letter has been sent off following her instructions, without salutation or closing. There must be a salutation for feminist organizations which is the unabbreviated form of Ms. "Dear Sirs" was suggested by several women.

GENTLE READER—Dear Sirs?

Miss Manners is shocked. But she is hardly less shocked at your disdain for the proper forms, "Ladies" and "Mesdames." She considers it a violation of female self-respect to denigrate terms associated with women and advocate the use of those associated with men. Surely this is the very opposite of feminism.

Miss Manners also finds offensive any suggestion that feminism requires stripping life of its little courtesies. A letter without a salutation is too curt for her taste.

Like "Miss" and "Mrs.," "Ms." is derived from the older and once respectable all-purpose female title "Mistress." However, she does not recommend addressing respectable people as "Mistresses" nowadays. "Mesdames" or "Ladies" will do just fine.

A REPLY

DEAR MISS MANNERS—Regarding your advice that "Mesdames" or "Ladies" are the proper salutations with which to begin a letter to a group of feminist women, I have no doubt that you know better than I what is proper, but I think I can tell you that these salutations, especially the latter, would be ill received, and I think I have learned from you that it is not good manners to address people in a manner they will find offensive or tacky. (I have not, as you can see, learned to avoid run-on sentences.)

When I write to such a group, I begin my letter with "Gentlewomen." It is clear, dignified, uses the term ("women") that feminists prefer for references to adult females, and is the exact equivalent of the term that would be used in writing to a group of men. I have never heard an objection. I hope Miss Manners also approves.

GENTLE READER—Miss Manners assures you that "Gentle-women" is a proper, as well as a clear and dignified way to address a female group and happily bestows her approval. But she feels obliged to warn against the too hasty dismissal of other terms of respect.

"Madam" (which has to resort to the French plural, "Mesdames") is the exact equivalent of the masculine "Sir," as "Ladies" is for "Gentlemen." Both of the male terms are in nearly as strong use, to show deference, as they ever were. By eschewing the female versions, one strips that gender of a form of respect, while allowing the other to retain it.

ADVANCE THANKS

DEAR MISS MANNERS—Routine memos informing employees of new policies frequently close with "Thank you in advance." I find this irksome, as if they were afraid that they might accidentally thank someone who had no intention of parking in the proper place or keeping the copier well stocked with paper. I should think that those worried about issuing an undeserved "thank you" would be more effective with "Thank you for your attention to this matter" or the like.

GENTLE READER—Let's quibble about this. Miss Manners shares your irk (she can hardly say she shares your irksomeness), but disagrees with your reasoning.

Indeed, one does not properly thank people for what they have not done—not out of meanness, but because it would be presumptuous. Contrary to your analysis, that is what these people are doing. "I would appreciate your attention to this matter" (or, in the still more corporate voice, "Your attention to this matter would be appreciated") is the correct way to add some graciousness to such a directive.

THE CLOSING

DEAR MISS MANNERS—When I was in grammar school, my teachers explained the differences between social or "friendly" letters and business correspondence in a matter-of-fact way. Friendly letters had a heading, a salutation followed by a comma, and a complimentary closing such as "Your friend." Adults' social correspondence might use "Sincerely yours" or another such phrase.

Business correspondence had a heading (unless on pre-printed stationery), an inside address, a salutation followed by a colon and, as a complimentary closing, either "Yours truly," "Very truly yours" or a very minor alteration of these phrases.

For years, these formulas served me well. Yet when I worked for the U.S. Government, my superior requested that I use "Sincerely." I also discovered that the government style manuals and the computer generated form letters used "Sincerely." Of course, I did as instructed, but found it odd.

When teaching legal writing to adult paralegal students, I presented "Yours truly." The phrases sounded so unfamiliar that the students interpreted them literally and found an almost romantic overtone in them. I wonder if I am too rigid. I know that letter forms have changed over the years—"Your obedient servant" is definitely not used any more.

I have concluded that this particular evolution may be due to the advertising world, which has filled our mailboxes with mass-produced commercials in letter form. Probably advertisers hope that using the format of "friendly" letters persuades the recipient to buy. A friend suggests that the constant dilemma of how to spell "truly" is another reason.

I feel awkward using the same closing for a condolence note as I would to order office supplies, so I persist in using the old forms. The recipients of my business letters may conclude that I am an old-fashioned lawyer (which is not a problem), but the recipients of my social correspondence may feel I am treating them in an offhand manner.

Gentle Reader—Miss Manners doesn't mind change (not much, anyway; what was wrong with "Your obedient servant"?) but agrees that the one you have noticed is a mistake. It impoverishes choice, as you explain.

Personally, she finds it galling, rather than comforting, to know that our government's idea of friendship is to inform people that their taxes are going to be audited, their military reserve unit has been called up and their house is in the way of a proposed highway.

Government, advertisers and others who write business letters would be better advised to maintain the dignified distance that symbolizes professionalism than to try to be cozy. They would also be well advised to learn to spell "truly," or at least to learn how to operate their computer spell-checkers.

Content

WHEN ONLY A LETTER WILL DO

It's a rough thing to say to people with a lot of nifty and expensive equipment, but there are still times when the only proper manner of communication is putting ink on paper. On certain occasions, a letter is the only way to show that you are sincere, which is sometimes necessary whether you are or not. Even without tearstains, there is just something earnest-looking about those wandering lines and shadings of ink.

It is also the only way left to demonstrate, for people who may consider that an advantage, that you know how to write. It is the only way left of proving that you actually wrote the letter. Or if not wrote it—because even a handwritten letter can be copied—that you are at least familiar with the contents. Nowadays it also deflects the suspicion that what appears to be an individually directed letter is actually part of a cleverly disguised mass mailing.

Business letters may properly be written on keyboards, of course, although it is not improper—just shocking—to handwrite them. Miss Manners has the habit left over from that awkward time between the demise of the typewriter and her discovery of how to feed real writing paper into her printer. She hates to abandon the practice, because it startles people so. And she knows from the trouble taken by her Gentle Readers who write by hand how honored one feels upon receiving such a letter.

There is still a rule on the records that all personal correspondence should be handwritten, although hardly any of it is. Even Miss Manners has yielded to the speed of other devices for the least formal communications—those that are only slightly more ceremonial than a "Hi, it's me" on voice mail.

But she holds firm on certain types of letters, unless there is a written excuse from the doctor which keeps the number down because the doctor doesn't know how to write either. Excuses from parents count for nothing here, as they may be responsible for failing to teach the habit of writing.

Pleas for the greater legibility of machine-made writing run counter to Miss Manners' experience that some letters are best misunderstood. The explanation for substituting a greeting card or not writing at all—the whine of "I don't know what to say"—doesn't work, either. Etiquette is willing to supply the message. It's the sight of paper and writing that supplies the emotion.

Here is the list of obligatory handwritten letters and their contents:

The love letter. Basically, all this has to say is "You're the most wonderful person in the world and I love you madly." (Miss

Manners is not guaranteeing that this wins hearts, which may take greater originality—only that it satisfies those who are already won.) If the paper is serious (which is to say plain rather than decorated with funny pictures or errand lists on the reverse side), the handwriting will not be harshly judged.

The condolence letter. Touching stories about the deceased are best, but failing that, the simple statements that the person will be missed and the writer deeply sympathizes with the bereaved are amazingly comforting.

The letter of thanks. The ingredients here are that the present succeeded in pleasing and that it symbolizes the kindness of the giver. Truth counts for nothing here and neither does the argument that it's a lot of trouble to handwrite letters when one has received a lot of presents. Not compared to the time it takes to select and buy a present, it isn't.

The apology. The message here is some combination of "I'm ashamed of myself," "I didn't mean it" and "I beg you to forgive me." This may not sound like much—and Miss Manners is not claiming that restitution may not also be welcome—but the fact of writing is taken as penance.

Extra credit. Letters of thanks for past or long-term deeds, such as bringing one up, being a valued friend or neighbor, or teaching one second grade, are not strictly required, but they are all the more treasured. A gentleman of Miss Manners' acquaintance reported that when his roommate was recovering from a stabbing, he did not consider the relayed message "Tell him I said hello" to have that personal touch.

Miss Manners is afraid that all these letters, valued for their appearance as well as their contents, must be mailed, rather than faxed. Along about the time of the invention of the postal service—no, not that long ago; back when the postal service was reasonably regular about delivering the mail, which was a while ago as well—there were emotional debates about whether using the mail was not too impersonal a way to send letters, as opposed to having them delivered by hand.

A Letter That Is All the More Polite and Welcome for Not Being Obligatory

. . . demonstrating that you don't need to go to the trouble and expense of personalized paper in order to be proper, not to mention charming.

Camp Dusseldorf, Germany

May 21, 2000

Dear Professor Marvell,

I was just going through some old boxes and found my 10-year-old paper on Oscar Wilde and Aubrey Beardsley. As I read through your nice comments again, I thought how lucky I was to have a professor like you. You made learning fun. I can't think of another soul in the department who would have let me serve champagne while I was giving my seminar talk on Victorian aestheticism. Thank you for everything.

Sincerely yours,

Duong Tran Awful-Nuisance

Hand is still fine, if you have one available. But if it's worn out from writing, it may just slip the letter into the mailbox.

THE GET WELL MESSAGE

DEAR MISS MANNERS—I had advance notice that I was going to need surgery of a rather personal nature (I'm 31 and required a hysterectomy after many years of pain and infertility) and thus had time to make arrangements for my house, farm animals and care for our only child. The mistake I obviously made is that I didn't take out an advertisement in the local paper.

I have received no fewer than 15 get well cards with messages like, "Get well soon. You could have told us about your problems" or "Get well soon. Why didn't you tell me?"

Many of these came from people in our small town (pop. approx. 800) that I might have met a few times in the grocery store or at church. These people barely know me or my husband and know nothing about our long history of trips to the doctor.

Please remind your readers that if they wish to send get well cards, don't add personal notes that may cause guilt to the receiver. I managed to control my temper long enough to write short notes thanking them for their concern and assuring them I was recovering well, without mentioning why I had surgery without telling them.

GENTLE READER—Miss Manners is trying hard to believe that the meaning of such messages is "If only you had told me sooner, I might have been some help to you in taking care of things while you had surgery."

She is not succeeding. If these people want to offer help, they could do it now. The wording you quote, with the ominous reference to "problems" and the accusatory tone of the question, doesn't help. Why didn't they just write, "Please let me know if there's anything I can do"?

Like you, Miss Manners is forced to suspect plain nosiness. That the old-fashioned variety, for which small towns such as yours were once infamous, has been replaced by the new nationally televised variety—bullying people with the accusation that privacy is somehow unhealthy—is not an improvement.

She shares your annoyance, as well as your polite decision to overrule this and address yourself only to the expressions of concern. She also thoroughly endorses your request that well-meaning people confine themselves to sending good wishes, rather than reprimands.

THE CONDOLENCE

DEAR MISS MANNERS—A fellow employee agrees with you that one should never, ever, send a sympathy card, because you are supposed to hand write a heart-felt sentiment and, if possible, drop it off in person.

I immediately thought about the three or four sympathy cards I keep on hand. Then I thought about the fact that if that is the case, can an entire division of all those card companies be wrong? If he's right, why are sympathy cards such big business?

GENTLE READER—Allow Miss Manners to give you something else to think about: If you keep sympathy cards on hand for whoever happens to become bereaved, how is it possible that such a card would have any personal meaning? In an already impersonal world, you are expecting a standard printed form to comfort people whom you presumably care about in the midst of tragedy. Even card companies sustain the illusion that their customers run out to find just the right card to appeal to a particular friend.

However, Miss Manners agrees that many people do resort to such mechanical responses, automatically mailing words written by a stranger rather than composing something personal, doubtless because they find it easier. Writing a letter of sympathy is hard. Etiquette makes it a bit easier by supplying

A Letter of Condolence

. . . which must be handwritten on white or ivory paper (in this case, traditional ladies' paper, a double sheet, 5 by 7 inches or slightly larger, and marked with initials, but it could be plain or with monogram or formal name and/or address), and for which "but I don't know what to say" is no excuse.

March 1, 2000

Dear Mr. and Mrs. Fine,

I am so shocked that I can't quite take it in. I keep remembering things like the year Phoebe and I both flunked Latin in high school and she made summer school bearable for me. We had a silly joke about "hic, haec, hoc" and all either of us had to do was say "hic" to set each other off giggling. She always understood everything. When I had a miscarriage last year, the doctor told me I shouldn't be upset because lots of women have them, but Phoebe understood and mourned with me.

I mourn with you now. I want you to know that Phoebe will always live in my heart. Brendan joins me in sending you both our deepest condolences.

Affectionately yours,

Harriett Grundy

The Reply to a Letter of Condolence

. . . which must also be handwritten on plain or marked formal paper (in this case a large single sheet, 10 by 7 $\frac{1}{2}$ inches, which can be used by a lady or gentleman), and for which being bereaved is no excuse for failing to acknowledge other mourners.

March 15, 2000

Dear Harriett,

Like you, we can't quite take in this terrible tragedy. But knowing that Phoebe had a friend like you and that others share our grief makes it easier to bear. We are grateful not only for your thoughts about Phoebe but for your generous contribution to the memorial fund at the college. It comforts us to think it might help other young women. Your letter meant a great deal to both of us.

Fondly yours,

Philip Fine

conventional words about being shocked and sorry, having appreciated the special qualities of the person who has died, and feeling sympathy for the bereaved. But it does expect friends to take the trouble to write out in their own handwriting these simple but important sentiments.

THE CHEERY CONDOLENCE

DEAR MISS MANNERS—A close relative of mine—young—passed away and a new friend sent me a card of condolence. On the back, in bright ink, was written, in large writing, "Have a good day!" I was shocked but also hurt. Would you comment?

GENTLE READER—Under the circumstances, this message is certainly revolting. (Miss Manners is getting tired of the word "inappropriate.")

But Miss Manners would classify it as more mindless than malicious. "Have a nice day" has become so conventional a signing-off phrase as almost to escape being analyzed for its actual meaning, any more than "good-bye" should be considered theological because it means "God be with you."

But watch out for this lady. If she starts predicting how long it is going to take you to "deal with" your grief, you will know that she is not the kind of friend to trust with your confidences and crises.

THE REJECTION LETTER

How do you like being rejected?

Not much.

All right, all right. Miss Manners acknowledges that this was a silly question. What she means is: If you are to be rejected by mail, how do you like having it done?

This may still be a silly question, but Miss Manners feels the need to pose it. People who receive rejection letters when they submit job applications or work that they are offering for sale are forever complaining to her that the return letters they receive are rude. These rejections are impersonal, lifeless and vague. "Thank you for thinking of us, but we find we cannot use you at this time." "We are returning your submission because it is not suitable for our use at the moment"—that sort of thing.

Stung, the recipient complains that the agonies of asking for professional acceptance have been callously ignored by a smugly employed person who does not bother to explain or advise. The deficiencies of the standard rejection letter are easy to point out when one is on the receiving end, feeling understandably disgruntled and having been given fresh evidence that the rejecting institution is incompetent.

Yet rejections are going to be made—the most altruistic establishment in the world can't hire everyone and buy everything—and a letter must be written. Everyone agrees that silence in response to an application is even worse, as it extends false hope. So what would an acceptable letter be? Besides "Whatever your terms, just let us know, because we realize we have to have you."

Miss Manners suspects it would begin something like "We are dazzled by your qualifications, and would give our eyeteeth to employ you, but . . ."

Or "Everybody who read your work was stunned with admiration, and it breaks our hearts that . . ."

So far so good. But what happens after that "but" or "that"?

There actually are rejection letters that are composed with some sensitivity toward the probable feelings of the rejected, which open in a similarly, if perhaps more subdued, optimistic fashion. But their writers have only postponed the nasty deed and must go on to say that they are not, in fact, going to act on those warm sentiments.

One type then gives a this-has-nothing-to-do-with-you excuse, such as "We're not hiring anyone right now" or "Our budget for freelance work has been cut." The other tries the this-has-

A Rejection Letter

. . . rejecting the idea that such letters should be warm and reassuring (thus leaving the candidate even more puzzled and indignant about not getting the job) but following proper form on business paper (which may also include telephone and fax numbers, but should not look too cluttered).

BLUBBER, FLUBBER AND TWIT, INC.
40 FENCE STREET, NEW YORK, NEW YORK 10040

March 1, 2000

Mr. Brendan Truly Repellent
29 Alimentary Canal
New York, New York 10014

Dear Mr. Repellent,

Blubber, Flubber and Twit, Inc., regrets that we cannot use an employee with your qualifications at this time. Should the situation change, someone will be in touch with you.

Thank you for your interesting letter and resume, which we will keep on file. On behalf of the company, I wish you well.

Very truly yours,

Barbara Flubber-Twit
Vice President, Human Resources

everything-to-do-with-you approach, suggesting that it is only the lack of certain skills or approaches that has nixed the deal.

Do these charm the recipients? Miss Manners regrets to report that they do not. The first dirty trick is to raise hopes that are immediately dashed. "Whoopeee!" shouts the applicant, pausing after the opening. Then the excuses are not plausible. If you weren't hiring anyone, why did you advertise the job, or, if you gave it away already, why are you not begging such an admittedly sterling applicant to hold on while you find something else?

The suggestions are worse. Puffed by the initially stated approval, the applicant is either prepared to argue the judgment—or, poor thing, actually goes ahead and fulfills the stated lack, only to return and find that this doesn't alter the decision.

At this point, someone always suggests the honest approach. Oh, sure, Miss Manners replies, knowing of old that the mention of honesty is currently the go signal for nastiness. Go ahead and write, "I tried to drop your letter in the wastebasket without touching it. This is about the worst example of ineptitude to come into this office. You must think we are crazy or you wouldn't be wasting our time."

Anyone who would write such letters (not having heard of the kind of nasty redress now sought for insult) is practically guaranteed to deliver one to an embryo genius, who will make public use of it throughout a brilliant career.

What, then, is left? Miss Manners maintains it is that very impersonal, lifeless and vague letter that has been so scorned by those with the ill luck to receive it. Those very qualities help one to avoid the pain and discouragement of having been personally, thoughtfully and specifically rejected.

THE BEGGING LETTER

DEAR MISS MANNERS—Here is a letter we received from a 17-year-old relative: "It is of course CHRISTMAS!! This year I would like nothing but money but if you have already picked something out for me that is fine too. Over the past couple of weeks my luck in rodeo hasn't (sic) gone my way. Just last weekend I lost $250 dollars. I've got a big roping that I will compete in and I'm alittle (sic) short on cash.

"My birthday is coming up in the latter part of January, and I would like just money for that too. Like I said earlier if you already got something for me that is fine but I need money very badly!!!"

We sent this young man money for Christmas after receiving the letter, because we weren't sure of the best way to handle this. My husband feels it's the parents' fault and that he doesn't know any better. I feel that at seventeen, he should know that writing a letter like this would be considered rude. We're not sure what we will do when his birthday comes. What do you think?

GENTLE READER—Miss Manners thinks that you have kindly consented to teach this young man that such a letter is effective. Rudeness is behavior that offends others, not that encourages others to be generous.

On his birthday, you might consider sending this young man a box of commas. He seems to have an urgent need for them.

THE NOTE TO THE PRINCIPAL

DEAR MISS MANNERS—At my daughter's parochial school, where the principal is as autocratic with parents as she is with children, we in theory have no say in the matter of which teacher our children are assigned to.

However—ah, the grapevine!—I hear that there are *ways* around this. Only no one seems too sure as to what they are.

Between the two possible teachers for next year, one is perceptive and creative, while the other appears to have all the imagination of a turnip. I know I want to write a letter rather

An Irascible But Polite Letter of Complaint

. . . which is duly logged in as an expression of public opinion.

P.O. Box 12
Harte Island, Maine 04852

July 31, 2000

The Honorable Chuck Appalling
Senate Office Building
Washington, D.C. 20510

Dear Senator Appalling,

I am writing you about your sponsorship of a bill banning deer hunting. You certainly cannot have heard about our problems here on Harte Island.

We've had deer on the island since the 1890s when they were brought over by my great-grandfather, who liked venison. However, the fact that neither he nor any subsequent hunter was a particularly good shot, combined with the extraordinary fecundity of the herd, has led to a situation where the last time anyone could grow a garden here without an electric fence was the summer of 1957. And even the electric fences stopped being useful in the early '80s when the deer learned how to turn them off.

The deer eat everything, including poison ivy, and the island has become a wasteland. They started breaking into the fish houses to get at the catch. Dogs and cats started to disappear and the bones of Earl Watson's goat were found out on Deer Point, picked clean. Recently lobster boats have gone missing for days at a time and when we check our lobster traps, they've been cleaned out. If the trend spreads, what is at stake is nothing less than the availability of surf-n-turf in the nation's restaurants. I urge you to reconsider your position.

Very truly yours,

Obadiah Jacobs

Obadiah Jacobs

than go in and see the principal, since the lady's mere presence reduces me, in spirit, to a stammering 12-year-old caught chewing gum in class. The question is what am I going to write. I don't suppose Miss Manners will allow me to call the less desired teacher a turnip, nor would it be politic to do so.

GENTLE READER—Miss Manners will help you, but not until you take out that gum and quit fidgeting. Do you understand?

(Sorry about that. When you reported stammering in front of the principal while approaching Miss Manners in a fearless and confident spirit, a flicker of worry passed through her that she might be losing her touch. It is gone. Please forgive her.)

Where were we? Oh, yes. Investigating the "ways" that parents can influence a school although it has a policy to the contrary. Miss Manners doesn't know your particular school, but there are some schools that become amazingly accommodating when people donate buildings to them. If yours is above such things, or your budget is below, you will have to rely on courtesy.

As you have guessed, it is not courteous to call someone a turnip, especially someone who may then turn out to be your child's turnip—ah, teacher. It is highly courteous, however, to praise a teacher for being perceptive and creative. If you write a letter of praise for the good teacher and add that you are thrilled that your child will be in that teacher's class next year, even an autocratic principal may assume that it would not be worth the effort to disillusion a happy and enthusiastic parent.

PEN PALS

DEAR MISS MANNERS—I wish to write to a queen, and would like instructions on the proper etiquette. The only things I have in common with her is that we married men from the same country, we are from the same country and soon I will be living in her country.

Is this done? My husband said that you can't write to a queen like writing to the president.

GENTLE READER—The proper etiquette for writing to a queen is to refrain from offering her advice on how better to manage her family, livestock or country unless she has asked you for it. Presidents, in contrast, are the public servants of their constituents, and may be presumed to want to know how these people want the country run.

But perhaps you only want to know the mechanics. The letter is addressed, on two lines, to: "Her Majesty/Queen Snow White III" or, in some countries, on three lines: "Her Majesty/Snow White III/Queen of the Forest."

The letter opens with "Your Majesty" or "Madam," unless you are also a queen, in which case it opens, "Madam My Sister" regardless of whether you are related; or if you are an *Alice* fan, in which case you may correctly open with "May it please Your Majesty."

If you share the queen's nationality, it could close with "I have the honour to remain, Madam, Your Majesty's most humble and obedient subject." But if the country of which you are a citizen happened to have revolted against hers successfully, "Respectfully yours" will do.

An Improper Letter That Only Makes Its Target Laugh

. . . and goes straight into the wastebasket or on the office bulletin board.

I ♥ GUNS
EARL WATSON
HARTE ISLAND, MAINE 04852

Hey Stupid—

Have you been kissing Bambi again? I can't think of any other way to account for your weird preference for deer over (armed) voters. But I guess if I were married to the person I saw you with on C-Span, Bambi might look good to me, too.

See you at the polls,

Earl

June 14, 2000

CHAPTER 6

THE GRATEFUL WORD

MAKING ALLOWANCES

Stamping out sympathy is not a task that appears in Miss Manners' job description. Persuading the kindhearted to stop making allowances for those who are feeling overwhelmed is not even on her list of Things to Do Today.

But would everybody please stop defending graduates, brides and mourners who don't write thank-you letters? It is not only mean old etiquette you are offending by taking this position, but all those people whose only fault is to have been generous. No etiquette violation seems to upset people so much as the missing thank-you note. You are not doing the beneficiaries of this generosity any favor, either.

It used to be only the delinquents themselves who tried to excuse their shocking omissions.

"It's my vacation," the graduate will say. "I'm tired of writing from having to do papers at school. Besides, I've got to go find a job."

"I got so many presents, I couldn't possibly write that many letters," the bride will say. "Anyway, I was busy with the wedding, and now we're entitled to have some time to ourselves."

"I can't," the mourner (who would melt Miss Manners' flinty heart if anyone could) will say. "I just don't feel up to it."

All of them then plead, "I can't think of anything to say."

The worst resort to the low tactic of blaming the victims of their rudeness. "If someone wanted to give me something," they will say with an amazing tone of self-righteousness, just as if they had never dropped hints all over town or registered in every store they could find, "it should have been because they wanted to, not because they expected thanks. The satisfaction of giving should have been reward enough."

Yes, of course. It is tremendously rewarding to throw a present or a kindness into the void on behalf of people who have neither the time nor the inclination to get in touch with you. It is so satisfying, apparently, that some people just keep doing it for years without getting any response at all. Those people are called "grandparents."

They are making a mistake. Those who ignore presents should be taken seriously and not troubled with them again.

The distressing thing is that some parents, who would be better employed drilling the habit of expressing thanks into their children, are instead sympathizing with their rudeness. Along with other partisans of the nonwriters, they will argue, "Oh, I know he's pleased, but he's really been busy," or "Of course she likes it, but you've got to understand, she never writes letters. Kids just don't, any more."

Among them, they have managed to intimidate the present givers, who either nurse their grievance in silence (well, not total silence—they do tell Miss Manners about it and mention it to all their friends) or pretend that they really don't expect thanks, but that they only want to know if the present actually arrived.

It's not true. That is, they do want to know that the present arrived, but they also want to know that it was successful in producing pleasure and that their goodwill in sending it inspired some return warmth of feeling.

That may not meet the high standard of selfless generosity claimed by the gratitude defaulters. But measured against alternative human emotions (for instance, such increasingly popular ones as "Who cares?" and "Why should I do anything for them?") it's pretty nice and should be encouraged.

The argument that letter writing is an old-fashioned habit no longer practiced is, Miss Manners feels obliged to mention, out-of-date. Since the blessing of E-mail, young people in particular have become accustomed to expressing themselves in writing. The technological adjustment in switching from computer to the pen and paper required for thank-you letters is not beyond their skills.

Miss Manners has made the emotionally extravagant claim that such letters benefit the letter writer, as well as the recipient. In general, she means this in the spirit of most good-for-you formulae, which means that the person who has to do it isn't going to like it. Nevertheless, it is true that being forced to focus on another's kindness is good for the soul and especially valuable to those bloated with good fortune.

However, the practice really does immediately benefit the unfortunate—those mourners, whose reluctance to respond to condolence letters, flowers, and donations is so pathetically understandable. Rousing yourself from grief to acknowledge that people share your grief provides real comfort. Acting on behalf of the deceased, in assuring sympathizers that they were highly thought of by that person, is one of the few satisfactions available to the bereaved.

OVERDUE THANKS

DEAR MISS MANNERS—I am told that newlyweds have three years to send formal thank you cards. My nephew got married seven months ago and I am still waiting. My mother died before she was formally thanked.

Now they have announced that they are expecting a baby. Would I be within the boundaries of proper etiquette if I wait until the child is three years old before I acknowledge his birth?

Would I be rude to break my own tradition (I send a traditional gift to grand nephews and grand nieces) and not send a gift? This would save me time, money, trouble and feeling insulted when they fail to acknowledge a gift, and save the new parents the apparent hassle of saying, "It got here. Thanks."

GENTLE READER—With Miss Manners' blessing.

Presents are meant to be a blessing, too, not a hassle. Generous people pay attention to the reaction of those whom, after all, they have tried to please. If their presents seem to be such a nuisance that the recipients feel it is best to ignore them, no further annoyances should be attempted.

Now—Miss Manners supposes you want to show your gratitude for her saving you time, money, trouble and insult. A nice present for her would be to combat that pernicious—and widespread—attempt to put the blame for unwritten letters on etiquette itself.

There is no such rule about having three years—or even one year—in which to write letters of thanks, and there never has been. Your nephew and his ungrateful ilk made that one up. Three minutes is more like it.

OVER-HASTY THANKS

DEAR MISS MANNERS—When we were sharing a cabin in the mountains with relatives for Christmas, my brother's children, ages eight and eleven, opened their gifts, picked up tablets with their names imprinted on the top, wrote out thank you notes and handed them to each person who gave them a gift.

My nine-year-old daughter observed this ritual and proceeded to do the same until I pulled her aside and told her that I would prefer she write her notes after we returned home.

Knowing what I had said, my sister-in-law told me in front

of everyone that a thank you note is acceptable regardless of when it is given. I stand on the belief that what her girls were allowed to do was not proper etiquette.

GENTLE READER—Miss Manners never expected to live to see the day when she would consider a thank-you letter to be prematurely written. But this may be it. What you are describing sounds less like expressing gratitude than issuing a receipt.

PRE—WRITTEN THANKS

DEAR MISS MANNERS—For a baby shower for a co-worker whom I know only casually, I used my lunch hour to select, purchase and wrap a nice gift. As the guests left the shower, we were each handed a pink sheet of paper—a xeroxed thank you note, in poem form, "written" by THE UNBORN BABY!

Not only was the poem sappy and badly written ("I'm sure I'll need some clothes, you see/For when I'm born I won't be wearing any"), but it was also the only thank you note we received. I can't wait to hear your thoughts on this.

GENTLE READER—Miss Manners' thought is that the poem isn't all that bad considering that the author isn't even born yet. It doesn't scan, but what did you expect—Yeats?

But perhaps it is not literary criticism you seek. The censure you want is for handing out prewritten thanks and in perhaps an overly cutesy manner.

You are correct that these notes would be outright rude if they took the place of a legitimate thank-you letter, which is supposed to be inspired by the present and the generosity and thought it represents—and cannot, therefore, be prewritten. But as an addition to sufficient verbal thanks, they are inoffensive, except, of course, to literary purists.

Unlike wedding presents, which are serious and always require a letter, shower presents are supposed to be tokens for which thanks expressed to the giver upon opening the present are sufficient. An absent giver would therefore have to be thanked by mail and someone who gave a major present, say the baby's first year of college tuition, would be rethanked by letter. You might want to consider such a present, in the hopes that the child's style will improve.

THANKING ONESELF

DEAR MISS MANNERS—At a large church baby shower I attended, I was puzzled to see a blank thank you note at each place, along with the dessert service. To begin the evening, guests were asked to self-address the envelopes and list our gift on the inside flap.

I begrudgingly complied with these requests, not knowing how to refuse. At what point could I have politely stopped cooperating and how could I have fought off the stigma of being a poor sport?

GENTLE READER—Poor sport? Not to thank yourself?

Miss Manners suggests you carry the point further by writing a letter to yourself, thanking yourself for all the trouble you went to, leaving for the guest of honor only the heavy tasks of reading, sealing and mailing it.

PAINFUL THANKS

DEAR MISS MANNERS—Friends and relatives sent gifts for my baby, who was born with a heart defect, and received a prompt thank you. He came home from the hospital after two weeks, but after three weeks he took a turn for the worse and was back in the hospital. I was still receiving gifts, but did not get prompt thank you cards written.

After two more weeks, my son died. I just cannot bring myself to write thank you notes, but some of the gifts were from people out of town and I wonder if they think that I did not receive them. All of the givers are aware that he died. I am perplexed as to what is the proper thing to do.

GENTLE READER—Heartbroken as she is for you, Miss Manners cannot say, as most good-hearted people would, "Oh forget it. You have enough troubles."

This is not, as those same good-hearted people may well want to charge (if they weren't so good-hearted), from an inhumane devotion to etiquette at the expense of compassion. It is because those who care about us, as your friends demonstrated they do by congratulating you when that was appropriate, deserve better than to have their kindness ignored. Tragedy sadly demonstrates the value of maintaining the support of friends. A simple note saying, "Even in my sorrow, I appreciate your kindness" would convey that.

THANKING RELATIVES

DEAR MISS MANNERS—I have had back surgery, and everyone in my large family and my many friends has been very kind to me. I have sent in expressions of appreciation—special cards and notes, along with a personal verbal expression.

This particular sister says, "When it's family, there is no need to send a card."

Well, I feel my family members are special! They take from their time and resources. Is there an etiquette rule on this? Your answer would either prick her conscience that she doesn't make expression of appreciation and could cost her, OR it could save me money and a lot of verbal expressions that I feel come from my heart.

Our family has a sense of humor and we all claim we have proper manners. Sometimes my sisters are neglectful: In receiving shower gifts or bridal gifts, they have not sent cards. Or for a dinner party, etc. I may be extreme, but I think they are too casual about this.

GENTLE READER—Just a minute here. Are you saying that you are going to stop doing what comes from the heart if Miss Manners tells you there isn't a rule of etiquette requiring it? Are you just going to stifle your bursting heart?

Of course not. You are just miffed because your sister, who doesn't do such obvious basic duties as acknowledging wedding presents, is attacking you, who are going beyond mere duty to graciousness, on the grounds of etiquette. Miss Manners doesn't blame you. She's rather miffed over this tactic herself.

So keep on doing what you are doing and too bad for her. But just for the record, here is the etiquette of thanking relatives who have already been thanked in person:

While this is prompted by just such a special effort as you describe, the letter should cover wider territory. Thus, it would not say, "Thank you for visiting me in the hospital, looking after my cat and bringing me magazines," although these deeds may be mentioned. It should be more along the lines of "I always know I can count on you no matter what" and "You did wonders for my recovery."

THANKING POTENTIAL EMPLOYERS

DEAR MISS MANNERS—On a job interview, I was interviewed by more than eight people in the organization. Do I need to write a thank you note to all the people I met, or do I send the letter to my original contact and cc: the rest? If so, what is the proper procedure on how to cc: someone?

GENTLE READER—When you talk about needing to write thank-you letters—and heaven knows that doing so occupies an increasing proportion of Miss Manners' life—you need to separate the rule from the motivation.

In social life, you must write thank-you letters because it is the right thing to do. As an added incentive, you know that Miss Manners will get you if you don't.

There is no strict rule requiring a thank-you letter for a job interview. There is just a presumption that extra-nice people have an advantage in getting jobs, first of all because they are so rare and, secondly, because they will presumably be nice to have around the office. So we are talking strategy here, not etiquette. Yes, you could write to just one person, thanking the original contact and saying how much you enjoyed the opportunity to talk with each of the other seven.

But suppose you do write eight letters. It will be eight times as much trouble—more, really, because the letters should vary in wording and contain some reference to each recipient. That is because one of the people is bound to mention your letter to another who will say, "Oh, I got one, too," until all eight have compared what you said.

This will persuade them all that you are not only polite, but hardworking and imaginative. Thus, you will get the job. And you don't even have to send Miss Manners a kickback.

THANKING STRANGERS

DEAR MISS MANNERS—My son was terribly burned in an unfortunate experiment involving gasoline. Strangers from all over the area donated money to a trust fund established for him and blood to aid his survival.

I have been given a list of all those donors. Thanking all of these warm-hearted members of the area would make writing thank you's for a party of 200 a piece of cake. The care of this child is also physically demanding, as is the care of his siblings who are just recovering from witnessing the tragedy.

Would it be incorrect to write a letter to the editor of the local paper to say thank you? Obviously, we could not afford to take out an ad or to do anything requiring an expenditure. It will be eighteen months of physical therapy before this fellow is "free" again to be a "regular guy."

GENTLE READER—Even Miss Manners, who is deaf to the pleas of brides and others who plead thank-you fatigue, admits that thanking a whole town individually is a formidable chore.

But although she does not object to the letter-to-the-editor approach, she would like to see it supplemented. It is no trivial thing to establish a trust fund for a nonrelative and it should not be dismissed in one public letter.

Surely there are people among your benefactors who have asked what they can do to help. Letters along the lines of "Mrs. Rockfort has asked me to express her profoundest gratitude . . ." would serve, if they note that the crisis care of your children prevents you from writing yourself.

THANKS FOR HOSPITALITY

DEAR MISS MANNERS—I was taught that one said "Thank you for inviting me" or "I enjoyed the evening very much," but you never thanked for a meal. Now I frequently hear, from people who want only to be courteous and appreciative, "Thank you for your delicious dinner." Am I out of step and is it all right in this day of fewer and fewer thank yous to express your appreciation in any way that comes naturally?

GENTLE READER—As a matter of fact, thanking itself doesn't come naturally, so Miss Manners admits to being tempted to accept what one gets without quibbling. Yet you are right that the focus of socializing is supposed to be socializing itself. This goes back to when one's cook was presumed to be responsible for the food, just as one's ancestors were presumed to be responsible for one's things, and so you didn't mention either. Nowadays, however, one presumes that the hosts like to be complimented for the results of their hard work. This is why guests should not announce their food likes and dislikes, hosts should not mention what goes uneaten, and gratitude should be for the event, not the free meal.

THANKS ONCE REMOVED

DEAR MISS MANNERS—Is it appropriate to send a "thank you" note for a second-hand invitation? A friend got an invitation to a party for himself and a date. He invited me and I went. I thanked the hostess before leaving for a delightful evening, but I thought it was my date's duty to write the note. Am I right or wrong?

GENTLE READER—Miss Manners is tempted here to trace the wrong back to the hostess. This would be a really futile exercise in a time when the secondhand invitation, as you aptly call it, is unfortunately common practice. By failing to establish that direct contact, the hostess contributes to the notion that she is not entertaining that person—she is merely allowing a friend to entertain his own guest at her party.

In making a ruling for this difficult situation which no one asked Miss Manners' permission to establish, she is forced to side with you. Your date is the one with the primary obligation to the hostess and he should write the letter not only thanking her for the party, but for being able to bring you, who so much enjoyed it too, etc. But for extra credit, either with the hostess if you happened to like her or, failing that, with Miss Manners, there is nothing to stop you from writing your own letter.

EXTRA-CREDIT THANKS

DEAR MISS MANNERS—When I asked my wife about sending a thank you after we were fed and entertained quite graciously at a Bar Mitzvah, she advised it was inappropriate for such occasions, just as we don't send thank you notes for wedding receptions. This brought up the inevitable question of why.

GENTLE READER—Just so Miss Manners does not appear to be answering a question with a question, would you first be so good as to ask her, "Why not?"

Thank you; very kind of you.

There is no reason *not* to thank people for celebrations following weddings or Bar Mitzvahs, also mentioning how beautiful, moving or whatever the ceremony itself was, and how honored you were to have been present. It is rather a charming thing to do.

However, it is not required because (to answer the question you really asked) the emphasis is on the ceremony and you should never imply that this was put on to entertain guests. The party, no matter how much longer it lasted or more trouble it took to arrange, is considered a mere aftermath to the more solemn event.

NO-CREDIT THANKS

DEAR MISS MANNERS—When is a thank you note not a thank you note? When we are hosts, we always receive a prompt thank you from a guest who writes things like:

"Dinner was gourmet, except your mashed potatoes were lumpy."

"The children were excited about the favors, but Andy's broke right after we left. It was poorly made."

"We enjoyed the games you chose; however, we all found the last one quite boring."

As a hostess who genuinely cares about pleasing her company, I find these responses hurtful. Are we wrong to believe that a thank you note means "loving the giver" for giving, and leaving any complaints unwritten is not an error of omission?

GENTLE READER—Oh, everybody's a movie critic these days. Your guest seems to be under the impression that hosts are eager to know how they can improve, and Miss Manners assures them that nobody is. Not even moviemakers.

Of course the purpose of a thank-you letter is to thank. What Miss Manners suggests might be best left unwritten and unspoken is any invitations you might be inexplicably tempted to offer this person in the future.

TRAINING THE NEXT GENERATION

How do you get children to write thank-you letters?

Well, how do you get children to do anything?

Miss Manners was once taken to task (and quite properly, too) for expressing exasperation that so many criminal parents seem able to force their children to commit unnatural and disgusting acts, while ordinary parents can't even get their children to say "thank you." We should not joke about degradation that defies all standards of civilized behavior.

Therefore, Miss Manners is the first to complain that the sin of ingratitude is being treated lightly. Gratitude and generosity must be firmly paired, so that we are always kept sensible of the human interdependence that underlies the premise of civilization.

Aspiring moral philosophers who argue that goodness is only goodness when it is indifferent to indifference should be congratulated for their thoughtfulness and sat firmly down with paper and pen. When they are finished writing all letters due, they may be invited to continue the debate by considering how a humble and saintly giver, who seeks no reward on earth, is to know whether his or her offering was welcome. Persisting in annoying people with overtures they ignore surely cannot be construed as a virtue.

Yet the greedy and/or childish often succeed in worrying the good. "I know that God loves a cheerful giver," writes a Gentle Reader to whose children she sends "very nice gifts, by registered mail," every year. "But every year I get upset when I never receive a thank you note or Christmas card from them."

Miss Manners loves a cheerful giver, too, but not a foolish one. To continue to throw presents out into the void is silly; if the presents were received (as the G.R. knows from having registered them) without producing cries of delight, she may assume that they were a nuisance and that the kindest thing she can do is to cease to trouble these people with them.

"I know that you would never do anything so crass as promote good manners as a way to financial gain," another Gentle Reader writes Miss Manners, to whom she then offers the following account:

"My husband and I have always encouraged our children to write their thank you notes early and to remember birthdays and holidays with a letter as well. Commercial cards were never sent with only a signature. My daughter went on to outshine me, faithfully remembering her aunts and uncles.

"Recently, the most elderly of these died and among her papers were H.'s notes. Later, we found that the aunt had remembered her most generously, which of course put the noses of the other nieces and nephews quite out of joint, H. being accused of being sneaky.

"Having read some of the letters, I believe that a genuine friendship grew between the two, and that all of the 29 cent stamps and 5 minutes of time added up through the years to a sizable nest egg. Courtesy does pay off, sometimes 'only' in courtesy returned, but sometimes in bankable dividends. Maybe with such a reminder, people will get back to their foolscap and fountain pens and relearn the art of the personal letter."

So much for motivation. But what to write (Miss Manners hears a high-pitched chorus whining from the desks to which their parents have quite properly pinned them)?

The proper expression of thanks must be accompanied by a vivid detail, as convincing evidence that the reply is not a form letter but was inspired by the actual and particular present. Miss Manners suggests adults prying such expressions out of children by interviewing them until some positive statement presents itself.

She has the good fortune to be able to offer genuine examples, offered by a Gentle Reader with the generous wish that "the cockles of your courteous heart will be warmed by the enclosed photocopies of some thank-you notes I have received from a friend's children over the last few years:

" 'Thank you for the creepy-crawly thingsamagigs. Believe me, they're gross. (That's why I like them.)'

" 'Thank you for the pretty make-up. I'm glad you had dinner with us.'

" 'Thank you for the shark food and the book, "Queen of the Damned." The shark food is delicious and the book is excellent so far.' "

The recipient of these marvelous missives goes on to say that she feels compelled to justify the choice of presents noted in that last note. It seems that the gentleman in question had previously revealed his literary tastes by attempting to abscond with a copy of *The Vampire Lestat* she had lent his parents.

By her next present, she had indicated that she had paid attention to his wishes. By the letter, and most especially by that cautious and authentic "so far," he indicated that he was giving properly close and appreciative attention to her thoughtfulness.

This is the ideal exchange, which makes the giving and receiving of presents worthwhile as a symbolic act of friendship, rather than a pointless system of taxation in goods.

So—what about that shark food? Never mind. Whatever it is these children have been getting, it seems to have produced in them a healthy appreciation of human kindness.

TEACHING INGRATITUDE

DEAR MISS MANNERS—I have an eight-month-old son, the only grandchild on my side. My mother is always buying him presents and I always write thank you cards for each gift. I found out from one of my brothers that she does not like this—she says that grandmothers are supposed to buy their grandchildren things.

Should I stop writing thank you notes except at Christmas and his birthday, since it makes her feel uncomfortable? I always thank her verbally. Is this enough? And what if this continues until he is old enough to understand that he must write thank you cards? Should I have him write to everyone who gives him a gift except his grandmother?

GENTLE READER—Your mother is trying to kill thank-you letters?

Tell her Miss Manners says she should watch out when she goes outside, especially anywhere near a senior citizens' center. Grandparents all over the country will hate her. They have been sending presents and checks for birthdays, Christmas and graduations for years and have encountered only stony silence in return.

Perhaps your mother is only indicating that she finds written thanks excessive for trivial presents, when verbal thanks have been given. Even so, she is fooling with a dangerous principle.

Certainly, you will train your son to express his thanks in writing. Being so civilized yourself, you want your child to be so, as well. Miss Manners can hardly imagine that your mother, who is obviously fond of him, will object to getting letters from him when he is old enough to write.

You should then teach him to write letters, however brief, rather than to send any sort of preprinted cards, and not to express the thanks baldly, but to imbed it in chattiness—not "Thanks for the rubber duckie," but "I had such a great time in the bath tonight with my rubber duckie you sent me."

REMEDIAL WORK

DEAR MISS MANNERS—I am a grandmother of six. Of my four children, three are incredibly prompt in acknowledging gifts for their children, something I taught all my offspring. However, the youngest and his wife acknowledge absolutely nothing from anyone in the family.

It is causing great hostility all around and my pointed hints do not seem to sink in. I hate to think of innocent children being deprived of gifts from Grandmother, yet I am insulted that no mention is ever made of what I do. I have a very limited income and the limits may become even smaller if normal etiquette is not observed.

GENTLE READER—By Miss Manners' count, you managed to teach manners to three out of four children, which is not bad. Although your job should be completed, perhaps your grandmotherly sympathies will bring you out of retirement to perform this task yet again.

You need not—in fact, should not—criticize your grandchildren's parents in order to accomplish this. Of course, you need not continue sending them presents, either, since they do not seem to appreciate them. But as part of your own relationship to your grandchildren, you can gently explain the dynamics of generosity. To give is a pleasure, but only if it is clear that one has given pleasure. It would be pointless to keep sending things to people who don't want them, or who appear, from their lack of satisfaction, not to want them.

Your next present to them could be a box of paper, pen and stamps and the offer to teach them how to write thank you letters by helping them write those due to other members of the family.

MEAGER THANKS

Dear Miss Manners—I sent a generous check to my 37-year-old grand-niece on her birthday and when I received my canceled checks, she had written "Thanks" on the back of it. Please understand that I do not send presents just to receive thanks. But don't you think she could have written a little note?

Gentle Reader—Of course; but why do you seem to be apologizing? Thanks are intended not only to gratify the giver (a perfectly legitimate desire, in spite of attempts by the rude-and-selfish to brand the polite-and-generous as selfish) but to indicate whether the present was a success. Yours does not seem to be much of one, since it drew such a meager response. Miss Manners would not advise you to repeat it.

BABY THANKS

Dear Miss Manners—When my seven-month-old daughter was born, I signed just my husband's and my names to her thank you cards. Should I pretend the letters are from her and sign her name? Or do I sign all of our names and thank the person for the gift for "the baby"? Would it make a difference if the card were to a family member, for example a grandmother?

A Thank You Letter for a Present,
Regardless of Whether It Hit the Mark

. . . gushed—although thankfully without smiley faces—on house paper (standard is $7\frac{1}{2}$ inches by $10\frac{1}{2}$ but it can also be somewhat smaller) which can be used by anyone in the house including (with permission) the house guests.

29 Alimentary Canal
New York, New York 10014

Wednesday

Dear Aunt Emelda,

It was so sweet of you to remember my birthday. The multi-color rhinestone shoe buckles are amazing. They give new meaning to the phrase "twinkle-toes." I shall think of you whenever I look at them.

Much love,
Harriett

GENTLE READER—Miss Manners has observed that grand-mothers do, indeed, tend to be more charmed than more distant acquaintances with letters that purport to come from infants. You are the best judge of who else is likely to be charmed and who might be revolted.

In any case, Miss Manners urges you to give up the practice when your daughter is old enough to write and begin the more difficult parental duty of teaching and nagging her to send her own thanks. Even a mother doesn't find it charming when she has to write the thank-you letters for her newly married thirty-year-old daughter.

CHAPTER 7

THE DELIVERED WORD

THE ENVELOPE

ENVELOPE FLAPS

DEAR MISS MANNERS—I was rebuked and embarrassed, at a dinner outing with my parents and some friends of theirs, when I was told that one is supposed to tuck in the envelope flap of a letter, rather than seal it, when giving a card to a friend.

I licked only the tip to seal it, as the card had to travel home with my father that evening and then to Europe with him a week later. Everyone seemed up-in-arms about it and my mother told me it was rude. If this is such a breach of etiquette, I wonder why she didn't teach me earlier?

GENTLE READER—Maybe she already taught you everything else—except that one should not embarrass one's children in front of others, which she apparently doesn't know.

It is true that one does not seal the envelope of a letter that one has asked someone else to deliver. The idea seems to be that you are so certain that the carrier is honorable and therefore would not peek into the letter, that you didn't bother. But this is such a fine point that Miss Manners would like to point out to your mother how lucky she is that your behavior is such that she can consider this a major breach.

STUFFING THE ENVELOPE

DEAR MISS MANNERS—What is the proper way to insert a card in an envelope? Should it be done so that when the receiver opens it he can see a part of the picture peeking out, or so that the blank back is facing him?

GENTLE READER—The back isn't completely blank. It probably has the copyright of the card designer and a code that anyone who has ever worked in a retail store can figure out to get the price of the card.

This is not, Miss Manners feels obliged to tell you, the information with which one wants to greet the receiver of a greeting card. The card is therefore properly inserted with the picture facing the back of the envelope, which is the part usually facing people opening their mail either by plucking up the envelope flap or by slitting the envelope with a dainty silver knife.

Large flat sheets of writing paper are properly folded into thirds, with the top third facing the envelope flap so the letter faces the reader when pulled from the envelope and unfolded. Small flat or double sheets should be folded in half, with the fold at the bottom of the envelope and the top half facing the envelope flap.

ADDRESSING THE ENVELOPE

DEAR MISS MANNERS—I wish you would address yourself to the problem of card-sending in contemporary times, when many couples are not "Mr. and Mrs."

Mary Jones may have lived with Amy for a quarter of a century. They socialize together in the great heterosexual world. They are accepted as a team. But the great heterosexual world has never learned—or listened to—Amy's last name.

Bob Smith and his friend Joe have owned businesses together and lived together for 40 years. Same problem.

There are also a Marian Smith and her long-time partner, Bill. But they are not Mr. and Mrs.

How should a Christmas card be addressed?

My 40-year partner deeply resents my receiving a card giving my name and then saying "and Bob." He feels it gives him the status of the family pet.

Is it better to receive a card from an old friend, well aware of the long-standing relationship (herself a divorcée) who refuses to mention the name of the partner?

My feeling is that the most tactful solution would be to address the envelope only to Mr. or Miss—to the partner you know best and whose name you can spell—and inside the card, which is the personal part, address it to "Dear Janet and Charlie."

GENTLE READER—The solution you suggest is an excellent one but Miss Manners feels obliged to point out that it is not the most tactful one—only the second most tactful. The most tactful solution is to learn these people's names, for goodness' sake.

Miss Manners fails to understand why this is so hard. When a friend marries, one has to learn one new name and often two, since the Mr. and Mrs. formula is by no means universally used even within the quaint world of legal marriage. Surely it is no more difficult to find out, over so many decades, the surnames of Amy, Bob and Bill.

When a card is addressed to two people who have different names, two lines are used, with the honorifics the recipients prefer:

Dr. Mary Jones
Ms. Amy Hawthorne

In a world where computers have the impudence to address people they don't know by name, it does not seem outlandish to Miss Manners that people could learn the names of their friends.

Addressing an Assortment of Dignitaries

. . . most (but not all) of whom have recklessly announced that they are always eager to hear public opinion.

SPIRITUAL INTERVENTION

ADDRESS	SALUTATION
✓ The Reverend Thomas Aquinas Grundy Church of Our Lady of Perpetual Rectitude 1 Peregrine Way Cross Station, New York 23456	Dear Father Grundy,
✓ The Reverend Cotton Ann Mather-Grundy First Presbyterian Church 13 Hawthorne Street Salem, Massachusetts 01234	Dear Dr. Mather-Grundy,
✓ Rabbi Moses Maimonides Grundy Congregation Olam Tikvah 4567 Singer Road Portland, Oregon 67890	Dear Rabbi Grundy,

99 Lamasery Court
Daramsala, Indiana 87654

July 31, 2000

His Holiness The Pope
The Vatican
Rome

Your Holiness:

In my spiritual quest, I find I am deeply troubled by the question of humanity's inhumanity to our fellow creatures, deer in particular.

GOVERNMENT ACTION

ADDRESS

✓ The Honorable
Chuck Appalling
Senate Office Building
Washington, D.C. 20510

✓ The Honorable
Robert Service Dauntless
Mayor of Lake Lebarge

✓ Vice Admiral John Paul Dauntless, USN
12 Spinnaker Street
Annapolis, MD 21098

✓ The Honorable
Daphne Dauntless Grundy
Dr. Gregory Grundy

SALUTATION

Dear Senator Appalling,

Dear Mayor Dauntless,

Dear Admiral Dauntless,

Dear Judge and Dr. Grundy,

Alabaster Mews
Hockessin, Delaware 47777

July 31, 2000

President Diana Hapman Dauntless
The White House
1600 Pennsylvania Avenue
Washington, D. C.

Dear President Dauntless,

    I am writing to you about your support of a bill
banning deer hunting and prohibiting the control of
deer populations using birth control pills.

ADDRESSING WIDOWS AND DIVORCÉES

DEAR MISS MANNERS—My sister-in-law, who is a widow, became furious when I addressed cards to her using Mrs. and her first name. She said people who did that were ignorant and should read an etiquette book. She says that refers to divorced women. I think she needs a new etiquette book—what do you think?

GENTLE READER—That she ought to read more widely in the one she has. Her book is correct that a lady's name does not change when her husband dies. But Miss Manners suggests that she spend more time reading the section on how rude it is to lash out at people who inadvertently make mistakes.

She is also incorrect about this being the way to address a divorced lady. This usage was briefly employed early in the twentieth century but was overruled shortly thereafter. It had been a reaction to the social drama that ensued when proper Victorian ladies who were divorced by their improper husbands refused to recognize the fact and kept their married names, to the (intended) annoyance and discomfiture of subsequent wives. Since about World War I, however, a divorced lady's name has properly consisted of Mrs. followed by her maiden last name and then her former husband's last name—if, of course, she took his name at all when she married him.

ADDRESSING THE UNKNOWN

DEAR MISS MANNERS—I received an invitation to a cocktail party from one of my neighbors, addressed to me "and Guest." This offended the gentleman in my life. When I attempted to explain to him what I thought was proper—well, the conversation went up (or down) in flames.

It is my understanding that invitations are addressed as follows: Formal—if a person is not married, the invitation is extended to "Miss Jane Doe and Guest" regardless of the fact that there may or may not be a significant other. Informal—flexible. Am I correct?

GENTLE READER—Not even close. But Miss Manners does admire the authoritative way you said it.

People who issue invitations are forever talking about how they want to "personalize" these events, but it never seems to occur to them that their guests could stand some personal treatment. "And Guest" or "and Escort" is never proper. Never, never, never! Everybody has a name and there are simple ways of finding out what these are. If your neighbors didn't know who the gentleman in your life was, they could have asked you. If they wanted to indicate that you could bring anyone at all, they could have asked you whom you wanted to bring and then invited him by name.

DELIVERY

THE POSTAL SERVICE

All right—you didn't get your check, and the court doesn't believe that you never received your jury summons. But there are worse problems ahead if the post office doesn't shape up.

Civility itself is in danger and not only because of the way people behave when they have to stand in a line that closes just as they approach it. Erratic postal service is embarrassing the polite and exonerating the rude.

Miss Manners is appalled at how unfair that is. It is not only that virtue (in the form of people who write prompt letters of thanks, congratulations and condolence, answer written invitations by return mail and send cards and presents well before the birthdays and holidays they are intended to commemorate) should be rewarded.

Worse is that the delinquents who have always blamed their delays and failures on the post office can no longer be safely disbelieved. It has become plausible that they did their duty, but no sooner had they affixed stamps to their charming notes and offerings than these were pounded, shredded and tossed into the drainage system.

Thus, the very people who maligned the postal service in its reliable days are now being protected by it. Now they can counter their disgruntled friends fearlessly, with such wide-eyed statements as:

"Of course, I loved your present—didn't you get my note?"

"No, we didn't show up, but, as I explained in my reply, we were unfortunately out of town that weekend."

"Why, I can't believe those letters of recommendation you needed didn't come. I got them out immediately; what do you take me for?"

And the truly wicked can turn tables with such sly inquiries as, "I hope the bicycle arrived safely—I suppose we didn't hear from Darren because he's been busy out riding on it."

Meanwhile, polite people are having their reputations ruined. They are suspected of deliberately sending invitations after the party to people they didn't want to have—or omitting some members of a family or social circle while inviting others; and of finally going lax, like everyone else, and letting those obligatory letters slide.

In theory, those with a good record should be given at least the same benefit of the doubt as the habitually rude. But Miss Manners has noticed that the socially meticulous are under extra suspicion. Exactly because they always did what they were supposed to do, they are now presumed to be administering slights of omission on purpose.

Miss Manners cannot allow this sort of thing to go on. She may yet break down and allow computer-generated addresses on envelopes, when the postal service claims that it is being bogged down by the cumbersomeness of handwritten ones (and never mind that dear Mr. Trollope, when he worked for the service, had everyone's letters delivered by breakfast the next day). She understands resorting to telephones, faxes and E-mail as backup devices—"Did you get my message that we'd love to attend?" "I was wondering if my present ever got there." "We suddenly worried we might have sent your invitation to the wrong address."

Nevertheless, she insists that important thoughts and important occasions will always call for hand-done mail. Now if someone would just please figure out how to deliver it.

THE LANGUAGE OF STAMPS

DEAR MISS MANNERS—Do you think using the Post Office's love stamps on letters to men might be misconstrued as what used to be called "forward"? Possibly this is a foolish thought in these liberated times. Please give us some guidelines on the proper use of love stamps.

GENTLE READER—Do you have one of those little stamps marked "Please forward"? Perhaps you could insert between those two words, "don't consider."

Miss Manners supposes not. She was just trying to save herself the trouble of sorting out the two very different questions you have packaged together here.

1. Do gentlemen read a language of stamps, the way people used to recognize a language of flowers, in which the sentiments of the gentleman could be read in his choice of blossoms?

Well, maybe. It would sure keep them busy rushing out to rescue maidens who happen to paste their flag stamps on upside down. Brides certainly think people do, when they shout "Love" from their wedding invitations.

2. Is it considered forward for a lady to send sly suggestions of love to a gentleman?

In liberated times, as in inhibited times, hints of love are only welcome from those whose love is welcome. Miss Manners cannot tell you how your suitors feel about you. But she can tell you that if you must express your love on the envelope, the Love stamp is preferable to a big old lipstick imprint marked SWAK.

THE LANGUAGE OF THE POSTAGE METER

DEAR MISS MANNERS—Two of my co-workers say that when sending out personal thank you notes and invitations, such as for birthdays or weddings, that it is OK to use the metered stamp machine at work. Two other co-workers believe that a stamp purchased from a post office must be used—that using the metered machine for such personal invitations is simply tacky.

GENTLE READER—Miss Manners' dictionary has not yet caught up with the current meaning of "tacky." What it has come to mean, when her Gentle Readers ask her to rule on such a point, is "technically dishonest, but so petty and widespread, and so tolerated by the supposed victim, that nobody thinks of it as a moral issue any more, but perhaps it still looks bad to a finicky few."

Announcing that one is planning to write off the cost of an obviously social outing as a business expense would be another common example. This not being the morals department, Miss Manners has to limit herself to the etiquette angle. The answer there is that yes, the appropriation of office materials for private use, widespread and unpunished as it is, makes a bad impression on honest people.

OFFICE DELIVERY

DEAR MISS MANNERS—I married into a family that I'm still striving to understand. My in-laws direct all mail and calls for my husband and me to his business. Keep in mind that I do not live at my husband's business and his family has our home address.

Not only do I view this as ill mannered, but 90% of the time my husband fails to bring the cards and such home and his relatives get upset with ME when we fail to respond. Recently, my mother-in-law faulted me because I did not respond to a birthday party invitation for our two-year-old nephew—but the invitation never made its way home!

When I send them cards, they call my husband at his business to thank US. Am I correct in assuming that it's bad manners for them repeatedly to direct mail to my husband's shop when I've asked them to respect our home; and even worse manners for my husband never to bring mail home?

GENTLE READER—Yes, you are correct in assuming that it is bad manners to direct personal mail to your husband's office and worse manners to berate you for not having answered it. But your husband's ploy of not remembering to bring the letters home seems to Miss Manners a masterstroke of diplomacy.

It is not necessary to get into an argument about whose fault it is or why they are doing this. You have only to retrain them by responding, "Oh, dear, I'm so sorry—the office mail just goes through the office. Heaven knows what they do with it—I know I never see it. If you send things to me at home, I promise you they'll be answered."

"OPENED BY MISTAKE"

DEAR MISS MANNERS—I have had letters addressed to me at an old address, opened and re-addressed, forwarded and mailed back to the sender with no information regarding current address. Presuming that a person has done the proper thing and notified the Post Office of a change of address, what are the rules of etiquette regarding those letters that insist on going to an old address?

GENTLE READER—Of course, misdirected letters should never be opened. It is as high a crime against etiquette, as against postal regulations, to open anyone else's mail (even if it happens to be properly addressed, but with the name of a member of your household on it, rather than your own).

However, Miss Manners is always ready with the benefit of the doubt. There are people, even occasionally including herself, who do not open their letters one at a time, but slit them all (with a nice old paperknife, since that does not chomp out a middle section, the way automatic letter openers do) before settling down to read them.

In such a case, it is possible not to notice that one letter in the pile is not actually addressed to oneself. The custom then is to reseal it as soon as the mistake has been realized—that is, when reading the salutation, not after digesting the contents—and to write on the envelope, "Opened by mistake."

Miss Manners suggests you drop a charming note to your successor at your old address, stating your new address and apologizing for the inconvenience of forwarding your mail.

CHAPTER 8

THE ENGRAVED WORD

THE FORMAL ANNOUNCEMENT

Formal announcements are baffling the people who receive them. Here is this piece of mail that came with the lingerie and software catalogues, the news that you have won several sweepstakes contests, and the bills: In a rather stiff way, it announces that (contrary to all reasonable expectations) a cousin made it through school or a neighbor's child has inspired more than a weekend's worth of love.

Why don't those who receive announcements of such events look pleased? "What am I supposed to do about this?" they wail.

"You're supposed to say, 'Oh, how nice,' " Miss Manners replies. "You're supposed to rejoice that those dear people have now been educated or married."

"Is that all?"

"You undoubtedly want them to know how delighted you are for them, so you are going to feel inspired to dash off a letter saying so." Miss Manners pours all the optimism she can into the tone of this statement, but without notable success.

"Oh," they say dubiously.

Miss Manners inquires why they seem dissatisfied with the definitive interpretation (the only kind she offers).

"I think," they each add darkly, "they expect a present."

That may be. But she doesn't like formal announcements of legitimate events to be classified as solicitations. These things exist with the artless idea that people might be interested in hearing what of major importance is going on in the lives of their friends and relatives. They are the grand version of calling people up and happily asking, "Guess what?"

For this reason, their use is limited to a very few occasions. Miss Manners approves of formal engraved announcements of marriages and graduations only and, in business life, of major partnership or corporate promotions only. She disapproves of formal, engraved announcements of engagements, births, adoptions, divorces, anniversaries, midlife crises, or conversions in religion, politics or eating habits.

The old-fashioned engraved, third-person announcement, which has survived into our own era, is charmingly dressed up in formality to suit the importance of the occasion. Because the form has been the same for several generations, it connects the event with tradition.

Yet Miss Manners keeps picking up clues that senders have doubts about what they are doing. Many who use the style nevertheless feel funny about it and find odd ways to undercut its seriousness.

Rather than understanding that even though modern life contains little formality, everyone is entitled to that grandeur on special milestones, they start messing with formal forms to make them seem more in keeping with the casual style of their everyday lives. They will add pictures in the margins, strip off the honorifics, substitute nicknames for formal names and switch from third to first person with dizzying lack of concern for grammar, much less tradition.

They take the basic form:

> Mr. and Mrs. Stephen Boosworth
> have the honor to announce
> the marriage of their daughter
> Alison Ophelia . . .

and turn it into:

Joanie and Steve Boosworth
are thrilled to announce
the marriage of our daughter
Ali-Oops . . .

Miss Manners happens to be fond of the traditional formal announcement and has never mistaken one for a bill from a friend stating that a present was due. But she sees no reason for people who find them unsuitable to send them to friends who don't know what to make of them. There is a wonderful way of making good news known to a lot of people at once, in which first-person, informally worded messages are entirely suitable. It's called E-mail.

ADOPTION ANNOUNCEMENTS

DEAR MISS MANNERS—I married a lovely woman who has an 11-year old son, and we have applied to Probate Court to have me adopt him. There is to be a hearing, but it will be a mere formality, as the application is already effectively approved.

I am very excited about this, as are my wife and John. We want to share this excitement with our families and close friends, who have already been very supportive of our marriage and the inclusion of the three of us as a family. How do we word an announcement of the adoption without seeming to be digging for gifts? We really do not want to receive any gifts—the adoption is gift enough for all of us.

GENTLE READER—Putting the question of presents aside for one moment, Miss Manners fails to understand why you want to send a formal announcement of the adoption to people who are as close to your new family as you have indicated. Surely sharing the excitement means telling them in your own words, perhaps even throwing a celebration. Even for the birth of a baby, Miss Manners much prefers the personal note to any sort of mass announcement.

While nice people will not consider this event a demand for tribute, many of them will want to show their delight in a tangible form. As you cannot politely head them off—any indication that presents are not to be given, however well intentioned, is vulgar because it shows the hosts were thinking about presents—Miss Manners trusts you will thank them graciously.

BIRTH ANNOUNCEMENTS

DEAR MISS MANNERS—I have always agreed with you that engraved birth announcements are pretentious and I could never afford them, anyway. But I simply cannot write notes to my extended family reading, "John and I are delighted to tell you of the birth of our daughter," because John and I have no formal relationship and these people have never heard of him.

Mine is a large and clannish family and, although many of them do not know that I am pregnant, this child will be important to its members as he will be the first-born of his generation. To write "Mr. John Beech and I are delighted . . ." seems incomplete, as if it needs an explanation which I don't intend to make.

Another problem is that John is not really delighted. He is surprised, if accepting, but neither of these go well on an announcement. I know that etiquette does not always call for honesty, but I also know that John would not take well to my telling people he is delighted.

I do not want to say, "I have had a baby," which only emphasizes the illegitimacy of the child. The thing that makes the most sense to me is a third-person announcement—I found some that are not cute and do not use those tied-on little cards, but are a very simple script on a small single white card. Their cost is within my obviously stringent budget.

I would have them printed with "Mr. John Beech and Ms. Laura Jameson announce the birth of their daughter," with her name, the date and time (but not the weight) and send them to family members and those friends who are not intimate enough to have telephoned, but who know me well enough that they would otherwise wonder if I'd ever had the baby.

I realize this is a very make-do solution, but I am having to make do in a great many ways now. I promise never to be in this situation again and when I am married and give birth to legitimate children, I will dutifully write personal notes, even if my maternal family has by then expanded from 50 to 75 households, which it may very well do.

GENTLE READER—All right, it's a deal. Miss Manners appreciates your attention to her little prejudices against announcements featuring a baby visiting card and introducing newcomers by their weight.

Nevertheless, she feels obliged to point out that no announcement of a birth, no matter how carefully and cleverly worded, will obscure from your relatives the fact that they seem to have missed a previous step in your life. You have even more faith in etiquette than Miss Manners—hard as that is to imagine—if you think any cleverly worded announcement can stifle their curiosity. Many will assume that you and Mr. Beech are married, which will cause some to pout that they had not been invited to the wedding, and others to worry whether they forgot to send you a wedding present.

All who receive your announcement will assume that you and he are at least living together. You will therefore be getting "Dear Laura and John" congratulatory notes and your closest relatives will be questioned—and question you—about who he is. His name will be written into your entry in all the family address books, for Christmas card and reunion purposes. In short, you will never hear the end of it.

So wouldn't it just be easier to write a short letter happily announcing the birth of your daughter, without even mentioning that someone else may have been involved? Miss Manners is not reneging on the deal. She is only suggesting that facing the resulting question of "Who is the father?" with a dignified statement of his name and the fact that you have sole custody is easier than dealing with it for years to come.

GRADUATION ANNOUNCEMENTS

Is it an affront to admit to having finished school? A lot of huffy people who have received graduation announcements or invitations to graduation parties seem to think so.

As Miss Manners recalls, the traditional response to such a mailing was something like, "Well, will you look at that—Sam is graduating already. Why it seems only yesterday I was bouncing a tiny baby on my knee—and now! Just think. My, what a lot of hard work and sacrifice must have gone into that. But it was certainly worth it. This is really thrilling news."

It's more succinct now. It's simply, "Why are they sending us this—do they expect a gift?" Sure. That's what everyone had in mind from the first day the child was enrolled: your present. Why else would anyone bother getting an education? It's that hope that you might toss over a ten-dollar gift certificate for the discount store at the end.

As a matter of fact, only a letter of congratulations is required in reply to an announcement, and spoken good wishes at a party. Graduation presents are lovely, but outside the most intimate circle, they are a matter of whether one is close enough to be moved to mark the occasion in symbols, as well as words.

Miss Manners is sorry to say that graduations are not the only happy occasions that inspire this mean-spirited reaction in the very people with whom the celebrants had hoped to rejoice. She has begun to worry that people who think that the answer to "Thank you" has changed from "You're welcome" to "Hey, no problem" now believe that "How much do we have to give?" is the new word for "Congratulations."

Wedding invitations and birth announcements are also routinely greeted by the favored ones as clever attempts at extortion. But at least, Miss Manners gathers from the complaints she receives about them, these are perceived as legitimate attempts. Even those recipients who are quick to point out that the news depresses them—they are not getting married, they are not having babies, and they are sick of people who are and don't see why they should have to fork over—will usually admit that these events were not primarily designed to annoy them. The people in question probably would have gotten married or given birth anyway. It is even grudgingly understood that they might want to let other people know about it.

Miss Manners fails to see why this minimally human presumption is not made about graduations. It seems to be expected that graduates should confine themselves to going off with one another to spend a night being sick and foolish and not try to involve anyone else. So much for the student who thought his or her relatives would be proud. So much for the parents who wanted to throw a grown-up party at which their friends would share their pleasure.

It is in the hopes of salvaging their innocent hopes that Miss Manners will run over the rules. The problem may be simply that they are going after the wrong people. Formal graduation announcements should be sent only to people who have previously exhibited interest in the family's milestones and had that interest reciprocated. That means you don't use the personnel list from the office, or the old Christmas list that hasn't been weeded in a generation.

The question to ask is "Would they want to know?" rather

than "Where shall I send this stack?" Perhaps "Would I be interested to hear that *their* child had graduated?" would be a safer question.

It is considered necessary to provide some clue as to why the recipient is being informed of the graduation at Medici College. One puzzled Gentle Reader reported getting a school's announcement without the customary enclosed card bearing the graduate's name or the least clue to whom he might know there. Another was thrown by receiving a graduation announcement from a classmate of her daughter's, as if she wouldn't otherwise know that the graduation was taking place.

A party presumes an even closer interest in the graduate. Miss Manners cannot explain why parents' friends who don't really know the younger generation are acceptable wedding guests, but only ones who have some acquaintance with the graduate should be graduation-party guests—after all, parents generally have a lot less to do with deciding on a marriage than with getting the child through school. But such is the case.

The saddest example reported to Miss Manners was a party given for a child who did not, in fact, manage to graduate with his class. "Unfortunately, he did not receive a diploma, nor did he get to participate in the graduation ceremony, but the party was still held," reported a Gentle Reader. "The parents knew in advance the son would not graduate, but didn't cancel. It was a big party, but the boy felt bad, you could tell, but it was not his fault."

Miss Manners is aware that the parents might be misguidedly attempting to build an ersatz self-esteem divorced from real accomplishment, as if the child wouldn't know the difference and feel like much more of a fraud than the guests. This guest reported that "we attended, gave a present, but did not congratulate" him. Miss Manners feels they should have wished him luck instead.

SPECIAL ANNOUNCEMENTS

DEAR MISS MANNERS—Our son will be graduating from university with high distinction—magna cum laude. The school supplies us with printed announcements which include a small enclosure card stating the graduate's name and degree, but since they are mass produced, they cannot state honors, etc.

Is it permissible to hand write the honor on the card under the statement of degree? If not, how would you suggest sharing the information with the many relatives and friends unable to attend the ceremony who will be receiving the announcements?

GENTLE READER—Special good news is properly announced in a tone of amazement, which a formal card does not convey. The milestone itself is told calmly enough, but any extras should be added on breathlessly. Thus, you might send out an ordinary announcement of your son's marriage, but if you want to tell people that his bride is a Nobel laureate in physics, you have to call them and breathlessly blurt it out.

In this case, Miss Manners will allow you to do it in a handwritten addition to the announcement, along the lines of "and he's graduating Magna! We're so thrilled!" She realizes that this uses up a whole family's allotment of exclamation points for the year, but heck, it's worth it.

DIVORCE ANNOUNCEMENTS

DEAR MISS MANNERS—When my marriage broke up, I notified immediate family and close and local friends in person or by phone. I wrote letters to out-of-town friends with whom I regularly correspond and sent brief notes to other mutual friends informing them that my spouse and I had split up.

As expected, all my corresponding friends offered their sorrow that things didn't work out. I never heard from most of the others, which was surprising in some cases, and hurtful in others. (Yes, I am assuming they all received my notes, but if not, they surely would have heard the news from mutual friends or from my ex.)

It got me to thinking if I had handled the situation correctly. If a written note was the appropriate way to inform them, what would be the appropriate response? If not, what is the correct way and how does one respond to that information?

GENTLE READER—You seem to make a connection between doing the right thing and eliciting the right response. Miss Manners assures you that any such bond has long been lost: People still pour out generous and correct invitations, for example, to ingrates who do not make the least response.

In your situation, there is the further complication of knowing what the right response is. That, of course, is what you wish to check with Miss Manners and she agrees that the traditional expression of regret, accompanied by kind wishes, is still appropriate. However—and that is why she inserted that prissy "still"—there has been an attempt to sabotage this.

In the understandable desire to keep up their spirits (or the less laudable desire to crow over another person's suffering or brag about subsequent conquests), many who divorce have been treating the end of a marriage as a cause for celebration. The "Hurrah! I'm free!" school of announcement has become so common that friends have become wary that even the most conventional expression of regret will be indignantly rejected.

Miss Manners does not approve of this approach. The dignified manner of telling or responding to the news of a divorce does not involve any discussion of the emotions involved. To trumpet failure as triumph is in terrible taste. And contrary to current usage, the fact that a statement makes one feel better does not excuse its being tasteless.

The correct announcement (not to be confused with the inevitable outpourings to selected confidantes), which is what you seem to have made, says merely, "Christopher and I have decided to be divorced," omitting expressions of pleasure or announcements of pleasures planned. A proper response would be, "I'm so sorry to hear that. But I haven't seen you in a while and I've missed you; let's get together."

CHAPTER 9

THE NOT NECESSARILY ENGRAVED WORD

INVITATIONS

Why should anyone bother issuing written invitations, now that the world is blessed with voice mail? Miss Manners' chief answer is that invitation cards stuck around the frame of a bedroom mirror ensure that the mirror always has some cheering reassurance to impart.

"All right, so you're not the best-looking person in the world," the mirror may insinuate. "But look at all the people who are clamoring for your company." (Fortunately, the mirror can't read backward. That's why it doesn't take note of the fact that most of what look like invitations now turn out to be invitations to buy admission to fund-raising events.)

Miss Manners can also supply practical reasons to put invitations in writing, such as having a written record of the date, time and place. She disdains to do so because etiquette only argues practicality when it has nothing more twisted to offer. In this case, it does.

Perhaps you are familiar with the etiquette formula by which the more personal a form of communication, the more flattering it is. For example, letters are better than greeting cards, and saying "I love you" in person is better than having a secretary call to relay that message. Well, with invitations it works the opposite way. The least flattering invitation is to say, face to face, "C'mon over any time; we'd love to see you." Whatever this offers in the charm of spontaneity, it lacks in sincerity.

Perversely, the most sincere, not to say solemn and flattering, invitation of all doesn't have any "we" or "I" in it. It's stiffly worded in the third person. Miss Manners doesn't have any rationale for this stunning reversal; that's just the way it is. But everyone with any sense knows that the "C'mon over" invitation isn't meant to be taken seriously, and that a coldly engraved request for the pleasure of one's company is about as serious as an invitation can get.

In most people's lives, the third-person invitation is used only in connection with weddings, Bar or Bat Mitzvahs, debuts or grandly celebrated anniversaries. It should never be gussied up with funny fonts, deckled edges or silly drawings; nor should it be dumbed down, with nicknames and no honorifics. The form for all formal receptions (a reception being an engraved party), a small dance (there being no self-declared large ones, even if the hosts have hired a sports arena), luncheons or dinners is basically the same:

> *Mr. and Mrs. Elmer Merry*
> *request the pleasure of your company*
> *at dinner*
> *on Friday, the first of April*
> *at eight o'clock*
> *480 Garage Lane*
>
> *R.s.v.p.*   *Black tie*

The basic information is here—time, place, what to wear and how much one can expect to be fed. There can be lines noting that the event is to honor a certain person or to celebrate a certain occasion. An absence of information about dress—which once meant that everyone knew to wear white tie and long dresses to dinner—now signifies business suits for gentlemen and dressy dresses for ladies.

Miss Manners is sorry about having to include that part

Mr. and Mrs. Maxwell Scott Nicely

request the pleasure of your company

at dinner

on Saturday, the thirteenth of September

at seven o'clock

The favor of a reply is requested   *Faux Chateau*
301-555-0915   *Steeplechase, Maryland*

A Formal Invitation *(above)* and
an Informal But Still Snazzy One

. . . either of which can also be entirely engraved or entirely handwritten, on stiff cards or double sheets.

29 Alimentary Canal
Apartment 2-B

for Harriet and Brendan

Ms. Heather Right-Megabyte

Mr. Daniel Service McGee

Tea, Sunday, April 27th

Four o'clock

indicating that a reply is expected. Of course, a reply is expected, whether it says so or not (and in the same form—Ms. Brittany Beam/accepts with pleasure/the kind invitation of . . ." or "regrets exceedingly that she is unable to attend"). What kind of dolts would imagine that their hosts don't have to know in advance how many people are expected to dinner?

Lots apparently, which is why it is more usual now to telephone around and send those who accept a formal reminder card:

> *To remind you of dinner with*
> *Mr. and Mrs. Elmer Merry*
> *on Friday, April first*
> *at eight o'clock*
> *480 Garage Lane*

Naturally, formal invitations are used only for grand parties. The next step down in formality for written invitations is to write telegraphic style on the hosts' informal or personal card—with the guests of honor "for Kathryn and Michael" written above the name, and the specifics—"Tea, Saturday, December 30th/Four o'clock"—below.

A fill-in card, either partially engraved or frankly printed and illustrated, may be substituted. Or, for that matter, a telephone call. Just don't come complaining to Miss Manners when half the guests claim they didn't attend because their answering machines were on the blink and the other half that they thought it was for a different day.

AN INVITATION TO PAY

DEAR MISS MANNERS—My fiancée and I are getting married in Florida and then, immediately following the ceremony, we are going to ascend on a balloon ride. The airfare to this event will cost $294 per person. We wish to announce and invite. Should we? Can we? How, if possible?

GENTLE READER—The airfare from the ceremony to the launching pad? The airfare to accompany you and your fiancée up in the balloon?

Never mind. The real lack of clarity here is your muddle about what it is to issue an invitation. People who are offered travel opportunities for sale are not wedding guests, even if the opportunity is to accompany a newly married couple skyward. Not being a travel agent, Miss Manners cannot say how one successfully markets that sort of thing.

AN INVITATION TO WHAT?

People used to give a "party" or, on grand occasions, a "reception." What they are giving now, Miss Manners has no more idea than their bewildered guests.

"Take a look at this," said a gentleman of Miss Manners' acquaintance, brandishing a written invitation. "What's going on?" The paper that Miss Manners was handed contained the names of three unrelated people, who were inviting the gentleman in question to "celebrate the newest phase in the life of" a friend of his.

This was someone he wished well and with whom he would have been happy to celebrate, but he had not been in close enough touch with her to be able to supply, unaided, the cause of the celebration. (He was unable to reach her for reasons that turned out to be connected with the cause of the celebration.)

As he did not know the hosts, he figured that the guest of honor must have supplied his name; and he was embarrassed to ask strangers a question that demonstrated that she might be reaching, in her guest list, for someone she didn't know all that well. Anyway, the request for a response specifically mentioned that a message was to be left and he got an answering machine when he called.

"Is she getting married?" he wondered aloud. "Did she buy a house? Maybe it's a special birthday. Or she adopted a child. Or she has a new job, or a promotion at the old one."

Suddenly he paled. "You don't think she's dead, do you?" It had just struck him that every funeral and memorial service he had attended in the last decade had carried the upbeat billing, "to celebrate the life of" the deceased.

Miss Manners is sorry to say that the gentleman ended up skipping the event, for fear that he might do something terribly wrong—show up with a present when a condolence letter was required, for example. "Even 'Congratulations' is risky these days," he lamented. "People celebrate divorce, or being fired and if you don't know that, you might say something awful." Only much later did he happen to hear that his friend had moved across the country. He had missed the chance to say a gala farewell.

Miss Manners considers that the many people who get invitations to share a couple's "love," "joy" or "commitment" are slightly better off than this gentleman. At least they may be fairly certain that the people in question are alive. But are they getting married? Did they skip the marriage but acquire a house or a child?

What if you wish them well and would be delighted to drink a toast to their happiness, but really don't want to be committed to sharing anyone else's love life?

A Gentle Reader passed on to Miss Manners an invitation she had received to a formal "Half Way There Dance" from a divorced friend and the gentleman with whom she was now living. "Half way where?" the baffled recipient wondered. Through life? Was she four and a half months pregnant? It seems that they left for the Bahamas after the party, but the starting point seemed to be the same as the party site.

Then there are the invitations to events that are called parties, but are actually "opportunities" to buy something one may or may not want, or to contribute to a cause one may or may not support.

"A Down in the Dumps Party!" one such solicitation stated. "I've been down in the dumps and I'm asking my friends to help me out. Bring a piece of furniture (see attached list for preferred stores and items I need) and a bottle."

Another read, "As some of you may know, I've long had an interest in the unconscionable state of poverty in today's world. I'm sure you've been concerned, too, but have wondered what you could do about it. Well, I've decided to act. I'm going to spend the summer traveling around the world, observing conditions and looking for solutions. You can help. I can't do this without my friends. Whatever you feel comfortable giving will be appreciated. Even $10 can make a difference!"

Miss Manners has no trouble with such items, other than the damage she causes herself by a quick smack of hand to forehead. The relationship they bear to invitations or confidences is superficial and misleading. They are fund-raising appeals and should be treated as such—rewarded or thrown out, as the person who receives them decides.

Even truly social invitations may be misleading, if the hosts fail to state that it is to be an evening of games, or that everyone will be expected to get into a hot tub. Could we have a little truth—and clarity—in advertising here?

The one charming exception is that an event for an occasion associated with presents—an anniversary, for example, or an adult's birthday—may be billed simply as a party. This is done so that the guests may protest, after a celebratory announcement has been made, "If I had known, I would have brought you something" in the happy security that they didn't. Otherwise, people should be invited to farewell parties or weddings or showings of the video of the host's recent operation, so that they will know what they are getting into—or may tactfully avoid.

AN UNNECESSARY ADDITION

DEAR MISS MANNERS—One of the most amazing—annoying—things people do to their friends is to put, in the envelope with an invitation, dozens of little glittery paper stars and other shapes. Almost inevitably, these pesky things find their way all over the place. It is a big nuisance to brush, sweep, or vacuum them up.

We started to enclose a few dozen of these offending "ornaments" for identification, but did not have the heart to do so; besides, we feel sure you know what we are talking about. Please dissuade people from use of these "cute" little pests.

GENTLE READER—Yes, yes, yes! Miss Manners recognizes a threat when she hears one and she is immediately succumbing to this one. She certainly doesn't want any of those nasties stuck to her rug, and she can't imagine that anyone else does, either.

But this is such a hospitably intended menace. The hosts want to spread merriment, which is not an impulse Miss Manners wishes to discourage in this grim world. They must just learn to confine the festivity to the scene of their parties. Vacuuming up is the last duty of the host, not the first duty of a prospective guest.

RESPONDING TO INVITATIONS

If Miss Manners were to decree it proper to have a line engraved above dinner and wedding invitations that said (in London Script or Shaded Roman), "Take this invitation seriously," she is under no illusion that it would change guests' behavior.

The following dialogue would still take place among the recipients:

"Do you think they expect a reply?"

"Nah. Nobody cares about that sort of thing any more. Besides, there's no phone number on it, so how could anybody reply?"

"Mine's only got my name on it. They don't think I'm going to go alone, do they?"

"I'm sure you're supposed to bring someone. Matter of fact, I didn't go to something like this last week because I couldn't find a date. I'll probably go to this, though, if nothing else turns up. I'm going to have friends in town that night; they'd probably enjoy meeting them."

"I do have something else I was thinking of going to that night, but maybe I can do both. I could go there first and then, if I find I've had enough of the first party, I can just drop by this one afterwards, if I'm not too tired."

"Did you notice it says 'black tie'? They're not serious, are they?"

"Nah. That just means something funky. But only if you feel like it. Nobody has the right to tell you how to dress."

"Maybe I will call, though, to tell them my food preferences. I went to one of these things once where the food was disgusting. No choice at all and nothing I could eat."

"If you're going to call, will you find out who else is going to be there? We might get an idea if it's worth going to."

And so on. Why would anyone want the company of such people?

The answer, nowadays, is that there are not too many others from whom to choose. Only Miss Manners has the luxury of limiting her social circle to people who are willing to make such major commitments as binding themselves to appear a week or two hence. Yet any social life beyond a spur-of-the-moment supper or excursion to the movies is impossible without a serious attitude toward invitations. And today's weddings and other major events are not improvised, come-as-you-are occasions.

So let's not hear any more about what guests don't have to do "nowadays." Do you ask your car every morning whether it expects you to give it gas "nowadays" just because you want it to take you somewhere? The real question for nowadays is how much prodding and nagging the hosts can politely do.

Guests should, of course, answer invitations definitively, immediately, and in the same style—written formal replies for formal invitations and informal written replies to informally written invitations. Not only does Miss Manners abhor "response cards," but those who use them report that they aren't working anyway. Delinquent guests are probably picking off the stamps to put on their bills, presuming they even recognize that they are still expected to pay their bills nowadays. As "R.s.v.p." is no longer eye-catching, Miss Manners suggests the formal alternative, "The favour of a reply is requested."

Social invitations are neither transferable nor enlargeable. A host wanting to know if the guests are part of a couple, or allowing them to form one for the evening, should ask for a name and send that person an invitation. Miss Manners has even invented a written form: an enclosed card saying, "If you would like us to invite an additional person, please give us the name and address."

An implicit, and certainly an explicit, dress standard should be followed. Hosts should indicate sensibly what they expect, with those who wish their guests to appear as jokes specifying that the occasion is a costume party.

Accepting an invitation means agreeing to meet whomever else the hosts have seen fit to invite and to make do with whatever refreshments are provided, skipping what is unsuitable, even if it means eating beforehand. But it is hospitable to provide enough variety so that those of one's guests with the com-

The Reply to a Formal Invitation

. . . the main thing being that there has to be one—a prompt one—and that not knowing how to answer is a pitiful excuse, because the answer need only copy the style of the invitation.

5101 PUDDLE ROAD
CAMBRIDGE, MASSACHUSETTS   02139

Professor and Mrs. Marvell
accept with pleasure
the kind invitation of
[regret that they are unable to accept
the very kind invitation of]
Mr. and Mrs. Nicely
for Saturday, the thirteenth of September

moner dietary restrictions—vegetarians, dieters, nondrinkers, observers of religious taboos—will have something, if not everything, there to eat.

How one mandates a general attitude among guests of co-operation, even if it is only to the extent of declining the invitation so that one doesn't have to be bound by other expectations, Miss Manners does not know. Should she allow the command about taking things seriously, she knows, sadly, what the reaction of those guests would be.

"Do you think this applies to us?"

"Nah."

R.S.V.P.

DEAR MISS MANNERS—During the Christmas season, we receive a number of invitations to parties. Perhaps you can clear up a discussion my wife and I have had about the proper etiquette required when you receive an invitation with "R.S.V.P." on it.

First, what is the actual meaning?

Second, what response is required for "R.S.V.P." and for "R.S.V.P.—regrets only"?

Do you call the host in each and every instance?

Please R.S.V.P.

GENTLE READER—How can Miss Manners not respond to your excessive courtesy?

That it is slightly excessive, you will understand when she explains that the initials (which the fastidious render as "R.s.v.p.") stand for *"Répondez s'il vous plaît,"* the last three words being French for "please." You have therefore asked her to "Please respond please." As Miss Manners believes that there should be as much courtesy in the world as possible, she is rather charmed than otherwise.

But please, please, please: Your response must be to respond. People who give parties simply have to know who will be attending them, unless they absolutely swear otherwise by using that admittedly practical but vainglorious expression "Regrets only," in which the host takes it upon himself to endow the reluctant guest with a regret he may not feel. However, you needn't always call. Sometimes you get to write! Unless they actually contain a telephone number under the instructions about replying, written invitations require written responses.

Acceptable instructions also include the straightforward "Please respond," or "The favour of a response is requested" complete with the silly English "u" in "favour." That sigh you hear is Miss Manners remembering when nothing was said on an invitation about responding because everyone who had any sense at all knew that hosts have to know who is attending their parties, so they just answered without being nagged.

THE MISSING REPLY

DEAR MISS MANNERS—I have, upon occasion, invited people who never RSVPed, and later encountered them in one place or another after the event had taken place. I avoided bringing up any discussion about their rude behavior and of course have dropped them from any future lists I have anything to do with.

Occasionally, I have wondered if there is some remark you have filed under Skewers, Stiletto-like, for Jerks Who Don't RSVP Invitations that would allow me to vent my spleen in a Miss Mannerly matter. Or is that an oxymoron?

GENTLE READER—Now, now, now. Miss Manners is in the etiquette business, not in the jerk-skewering business. Dropping them socially is about as severe a punishment as a mannerly person can offer an unmannerly one.

But if you were to say, "I'm so sorry to have missed you Saturday—I trust you weren't seriously ill," she would be willing to classify this as polite concern, rather than sarcasm, if you promised to say it in very even tones.

CHAPTER 10

THE PREPRINTED WORD

Theory and Practice

The antipathy Miss Manners harbors for printed greeting cards as a method of social communication is not, she is aware, widely shared. Others are apparently moved to tears at the thought behind the words "Thank You" or "Deepest Sympathy" stamped out in silver script.

Perhaps they should be. It is certainly true that finding and buying a preprinted card is a lot more trouble and expense than pulling out a piece of paper at home and writing the same words in one's own dear little slanting hand. And this is a society which believes that an act of consumerism—selecting a ready-made product and purchasing it—is more creative, more meaningful, even more personal, than the amateur act of improvising from one's own brain, if not heart.

Oh, grouse, grouse, grouse. The plain truth of it is that Miss Manners is disgruntled that etiquette, which is constantly being accused of taking simple tasks and making them time-consuming and expensive, is ignored, if not chastised, when promoting simplicity and economy. Is that fair?

She has been known to bolster this grudge with the declaration that no stranger, however professionally talented, can be expected to understand the particular conditions that may arise in the lives of one's intimates and thus tell them what they want to hear, in the way someone who actually cares about these people could do.

When she calms down and thinks it over, she is now forced to acknowledge that the opposite may be true. Greeting card companies have expanded their interest from the standard calendar holidays and cycle of life's milestones to meet the challenge. It would be hard to imagine a possible human condition that they have missed.

Do you want to assure your father's ex-wife that even though your mother blames her for breaking up her marriage, you never have held it against her, and even though she has now left your Dad's life, you don't consider that she has vacated her special place in your own heart, and congratulations for winning the state lottery?

Do you want to console a friend by saying that a conviction in lower court isn't really important, because a higher court is bound to overturn it, and while you're sorry you couldn't come up with bail, it doesn't mean you don't care?

Do you want to wish success to someone in search of long-lost biological parents, expressing the hope that they will turn out to be the sort of people who are worth such an effort, or at least won't slam the door and deny any connection?

Do you want to encourage loved ones whose house has been pummeled on successive occasions by hurricane, volcano, earthquake, flood and mud slides to look on the bright side and laugh about it?

No doubt anyone who searched hard enough would be able to find a card delineating each of these situations and articulating sentiments to go with them. Some of the approaches taken may not be appreciated by the recipients, but who says that the original sentiments that people express on their own always succeed?

It is exactly that fear of saying the wrong thing in a delicate situation that encourages the sending of cards instead. Miss Manners has to admit that the fear is justified.

This is because the underlying assumptions of our time are that anything that seems wonderful probably has a dark side to it and that anything awful was avoidable. People routinely express this by telling newly engaged or married couples about the likelihood of divorce, prospective parents about the likelihood of physical problems in babies and psychological ones as they grow, and they lecture the ill on not having a positive attitude toward their disease and help the bereaved mourn by attributing death to bad habits.

You would think that Miss Manners would be relieved to have these dangers averted by turning over the job to professionals. But no, she still has to insist on the appearance of doing it oneself.

Etiquette does provide help here. What it provides is a whole catalogue of things to say on every occasion: congratulations, thank you, I'm so sorry, happy birthday, I love you, happy holidays, best wishes and I offer you my sympathy.

None of these, it will be noticed, is funny, insightful or original. Surprisingly enough, that is not what is wanted. On important occasions, people don't necessarily want to be lectured, enlightened or kidded; they just want to bask in the idea that people who care about them are sharing their pleasures or sorrows.

Signing one's name to such a statement is supposed to convey that. Actually putting it into one's own handwriting suggests that there was some thinking going on, as opposed to mere acquiescence in someone else's statement.

SIGNING CARDS

DEAR MISS MANNERS—I say that any greeting card should be signed by me and my wife separately. She says no—that one of us can sign for both and that it doesn't matter. I feel that the recipient does check the signatures and may feel slighted if both have not signed. Not important perhaps, but you'd be surprised at the friction this causes.

GENTLE READER—Miss Manners is never surprised at friction over small points. The smaller the point, in fact, the more imaginatively it may be worked up into a crisis.

In this case, you are both right in that either solution is acceptable. But Miss Manners sides with your wife, not only because it is the more usual way of signing cards from couples, but because you falsely maintain that it is wrong.

Theories abound about whether the formula is "ladies first" or the opposite as it follows the "Mr. and Mrs." order. The answer is neither. It follows the modesty principle, by which the person who actually does the signing puts the other person's name first.

GROUP CARDS

DEAR MISS MANNERS—What is Miss Manners' opinion of the "group" greeting card, the kind that is "from the gang at Harry's" or whatever? I recently signed a get-well card of this description, but sent a note of my own the next day. I know that Miss Manners hates condolence cards, but what about group ones? How can one refuse to sign one without seeming to call the others rude?

What about joint gifts of flowers? Is it all right to refuse to contribute? (Once I contributed money but refused to sign the card; I sent a condolence letter of my own.) Suppose a co-worker who has made it clearly known that she dislikes you loses a relative? Is it kinder to send nothing? Since she is inevitably the sender of the group condolence card, no one is sending her one, to sign or not sign.

GENTLE READER—Just a minute here. Before Miss Manners answers your question about individual acknowledgments, let her see if she understands the current situation. The one person who has been tending to everyone else's losses is having her own bereavement ignored because no one else is willing to bother with the task; is that it?

That is pretty mean. Miss Manners is not crazy about group efforts, preferring individual ones, as you do, but obviously the lady concerned does believe them worthwhile, or she wouldn't have been organizing them. The decent thing for you to do in this case would therefore be to organize such a project, whether you like the lady or not.

In other cases, you need not participate in group cards or collections when you are sending your own letter. "Thanks, but I think I'll write her myself" is enough of an explanation to offer, but then Miss Manners considers you on your honor to do so.

DEMANDING CARDS

DEAR MISS MANNERS—I am the married mother of a three-year-old daughter who is the only grandchild on both sides. Is it not appropriate for me to receive Mother's Day cards from both sets of our parents?

I continue to purchase cards and gifts at all holidays for all family members, but I only receive a Mother's Day card from my daughter. Doesn't this seem to be a rather one-sided perspective? Surely I perform the same roles that our mothers did.

GENTLE READER—Come again? One baby and you figure you are mother to the world? Even to your own mother and your mother-in-law?

Of course it's one-sided. This is not Daughter or Daughter-in-Law Day; nor is it World Salute to Everyone Who Has Given

Birth Day. While there is nothing wrong with acknowledging and honoring the motherhood of ladies other than those who have happened to rear you, there is something awfully wrong with expecting this tribute from those you have not happened to rear.

ACKNOWLEDGING CARDS

DEAR MISS MANNERS—I love my 43-year-old daughter very, very much and I always remember her with a special card on special occasions. She has yet to acknowledge receiving them, so this last time I asked her about the card. She didn't know it was necessary to acknowledge cards. I really don't expect thanks. Just did she get them, the postal service being what it is, though a thank you would be nice.

Do I expect too much? She had a good example growing up. My generation acknowledged anything that was done to give us pleasure.

GENTLE READER—Technically, your daughter is right. A printed card that is merely signed—no matter how lovingly it was selected—is a minimal greeting and does not require an answer, as does a real letter.

But there is an overriding rule that one should try to please people who mean well, especially one's mother. Miss Manners doesn't often allow subgroups to make up their own rules, but if you wished to tell your daughter that you would like your cards acknowledged, regardless of the general rules, Miss Manners would support you.

COMMERCIALLY INSPIRED CARDS

DEAR MISS MANNERS—I want to send our clients Thanksgiving greeting cards, but my supervisor is concerned that Thanksgiving cards are not the "norm" and he prefers that I send Christmas cards instead. I feel that everyone sends Christmas cards.

GENTLE READER—Right. That is why they are sent.

Miss Manners mustn't be churlish. No doubt, most people send Christmas cards in order to offer greetings and kind wishes to those about whom they care. But among business acquaintances, a sender's desire to call attention to commercial services being offered has sometimes been known to replace the gentler sentiments. From your argument, that is what you wish. You would be right about catching the attention of those who did not expect to be the targets of a new custom.

Whether it would be favorable attention is another question. Miss Manners believes that businesspeople are seduced by commercially motivated social attentions far less than is imagined by those who approve the expense accounts. Christmas cards are common enough for there to be some room for imagining that professional associates also harbor kind wishes. Your invention of a new custom is far more likely to be perceived as a new gimmick or, if it catches on, a new burden.

CHRISTMAS CARD COMPLAINTS

Is it too much to expect people to harbor goodwill while they are in the very act of sending or receiving Christmas cards?

What has prompted Miss Manners to ask such a grumpy question is a letter from a Gentle Reader complaining that "people who should know better" are adding handwritten salutations, " 'Dear Ted & Marie' on the upper left, and the date on the upper right side of Christmas cards, as you would a personal letter. We were taught that a neat signature at the bottom of the printed greeting was all you should do."

How's that? They are greeting people by name, in their very

own handwriting, instead of leaving the preprinted message to stand alone? Outrageous.

A Christmas card, Miss Manners would have thought in the naïve days before hordes of huffy people told her otherwise, could do no harm. A simple greeting, from one person or household to another, may not live up to its announced intention of spreading joy, which is a fairly big order, but it could hardly offend. Ha! (As opposed to Ho!)

Even the envelope offends people, before the recipient has opened the card. Try as Christmas card senders may to abide by their friends' choice of names and titles—and indeed, they should have jotted down any clues they received in last year's mail—some of them are bound to guess wrong.

It is the unfortunate liberty of our times, in which such elementary matters are no longer standardized, that has led to this sorry state of affairs. Miss Manners doesn't much care whether the Mr. and Mrs. system prevails over the Ms. and separate surname system, so long as a standard emerges that people take for granted, rather than analyze for insult.

In the meantime, the rule is to follow whatever you know about the people you address, and hope for the best.

For example, a typical American family, where the parents aren't married and the children derive from previous social events, would be addressed as:

> Dr. Ruth Land
> Mr. Wayne Fill
> Master Max Margin
> Ms. Brittany Land-Margin
> Miss Emily Land-Fill

But if they receive a card addressed to Mr. and Mrs. Wayne Fill and inside it merely says, "Merry Christmas to all of you," they are not to fume that the senders did it to be nasty. Nastiness is just not a major inspiration for Christmas cards.

Their card could be signed "Ruth Land and Wayne Fill, Max, Brittany and Emily," but, for the purpose of spreading the word, the children's full names could also be given.

KINDLY GREETINGS

DEAR MISS MANNERS—Do I continue to send a Christmas card to my sister, when we have no meaningful relationship? We live 15 miles apart, but do not see each other or communicate in any way throughout the year.

I feel like a hypocrite every year, sending a card to someone who I know has very little regard for me. Should I stop the ritual or continue?

GENTLE READER—Pray, what are Christmas cards for, if not to extend a kindly greeting, to those who deserve it or not, in the season of forgiveness?

RESPECTING RELIGIOUS DIFFERENCES

DEAR MISS MANNERS—Not being of the Christian faith but having many friends who are, I always send Christmas cards to my Christian friends. My dilemma is that I receive Christmas cards in return, some with a very religious picture and message. I must admit that I am a little resentful and somewhat hurt that the consideration I show for them on celebrating their religious Christmas observance is not reciprocated on the observance of Hanukkah.

How can I convey to these dear friends that I would rather not receive any card at all than to receive a Christmas card for a holiday I do not observe? I am certainly thrilled and most appreciative of those friends who do remember my holiday and send me an appropriate card.

GENTLE READER—Your friends may not be callous so much as confused, Miss Manners surmises. The idea of sending people greetings on their religious holidays, rather than one's own, may make sense, but it doesn't happen to be the general custom.

American Jews have a wide variety of approaches to Christmas customs, from total nonparticipation to partial participation in the nonreligious aspects, to the adaptation of Christmas customs to Hanukkah (such as the sending of Hanukkah cards).

Because you send Christmas cards, your Christian friends assume that you are participating in this exchange. Those who know you are Jewish and yet send you religious cards are, Miss Manners agrees, insensitive. But those who failed to send you Hanukkah cards may actually be sensitive to the fact that some Jews regard them as an offensive aping of Christian customs.

THE GENEROUS SPIRIT

Miss Manners can afford to be calm about not planning ahead for the holidays because her own personalized cards need no advance work at all, even though they are instantly available exactly when she needs to send them out. They are personalized with her own little quill pen, with which it is only necessary to write "Merry Christmas," "Happy Holidays," "We've been thinking of you," or whatever simple sentiment applies to that particular occasion and person.

However, Miss Manners has come to realize that she is getting smug on the subject of frankly mass-produced Christmas greetings, an attitude that, while not actually impolite, tends to nudge one into the wrong direction. Fortified by the righteousness that her method is inexpensive as well as genuinely personal, she has allowed herself to share the indignation, sometimes laced with hilarity, of those who sneer at the preprinted greetings they receive, whether they are the printed-name-only variety, or what is still known, in spite of vast technological advances, as the mimeographed Christmas letter.

She still believes that the too-many-friends excuse is a poor one. What people who claim that generally mean is that they have ahold of too many people's addresses. Friends require at least minimal upkeep. Some may good-naturedly retain their status during periods of suspended activity, making do with a very occasional gesture and holding themselves ready to take up the friendship when the opportunity or next phase of life presents itself. If a greeting and a signature once a year are too much to spare these treasures, Miss Manners suggests that they no longer be counted as friends, which should trim the list down to manageable size.

Yet Miss Manners has been softened by the excellent examples of two Gentle Readers who took gentle issue with the custom of complaining about other people's efforts.

"Those readers who forward to you complaints on their Christmas cards seem to forget that a gift—whether a card or package—is still an expression of the giver and, as such, should be received in like spirit," wrote one. "As Voltaire once said, 'By appreciation, we make excellence in others our own property.' It is also true that by appreciation, we shall see excellence in others."

"Personally, I appreciate any cards I get," wrote the other. "I am so tired of hearing everyone's complaint about receiving certain Christmas cards—nothing is ever good enough. We no longer live in our home town and most of my old friends have moved away. Sometimes this is the one contact I have with them for the entire year. I do care if they have been ill, I do want to know what their year has been like. Send me a note, a letter, a form letter, it doesn't matter. What does matter is that they thought of me and included me in their circle of friends. When I receive a card with no personal touches, I consider it a 'Christmas greeting.' Wasn't that what it was all about when the custom started? If it is someone I would like a letter from, then I write them a letter and hope they respond."

THE LAST WORD

DEAR MISS MANNERS—Where should the author sign a book—on the first, blank page, or the first title page, or the second title page beneath the author's printed name? Also, in inscribing a book to a relative or friend, should the author sign only his first name or his full name?

GENTLE READER—Unless you believe that your full autograph is going to be your relative's or friend's fortune when it hits the literary auction market, you sign the book, as you would a letter, by the name that person calls you. The right place to autograph a book is on the dedication page. Other authors may tell you otherwise—indeed, some of them have been cheeky enough to tell Miss Manners otherwise—but Miss Manners is the final authority.

INDEX

ABOUT THE AUTHOR

Miss Manners' newspaper column is internationally syndicated. Judith Martin is the author of the best-selling *Miss Manners Rescues Civilization, Miss Manners' Guide for the Turn-of-the-Millennium, Miss Manners' Guide to Rearing Perfect Children, Miss Manners' Guide to Excruciatingly Correct Behavior, Miss Manners on (Painfully Proper) Weddings,* and *Common Courtesy,* as well as two novels, *Gilbert* and *Style and Substance.* She and her husband, a scientist and playwright, live in Washington, D.C. They have two children.